WEB OF INIQUITY
THE ENTANGLING OF SINS

BRIAN R. HAND

JOURNEYFORTH

ACADEMIC

GREENVILLE, SOUTH CAROLINA

Library of Congress Cataloging-in-Publication Data

Names: Hand, Brian R., 1975- author.

Title: Web of iniquity : the entangling of sins / Brian R. Hand.

Description: Greenville : JourneyForth Academic, 2016. | Includes
 bibliographical references and index.

Identifiers: LCCN 2016022023 (print) | LCCN 2016023002 (ebook) | ISBN
 9781628562811 (perfect bound pbk. : alk. paper) | ISBN 9781628562804
 (ebook)

Subjects: LCSH: Deadly sins. | Sin--Christianity.

Classification: LCC BV4626 .H35 2016 (print) | LCC BV4626 (ebook) | DDC
 241/.3--dc23

LC record available at https://lccn.loc.gov/2016022023

Web of Iniquity: The Entangling of Sins
Brian Hand, PhD

Cover design by NaEun Hyun
Page layout by Michael Boone

©2016 BJU Press
Greenville, South Carolina 29614
JourneyForth Academic is a division of BJU Press.
Printed in the United States of America
All rights reserved

ISBN 978-1-62856-281-1
15 14 13 12 11 10 9 8 7 6 5 4 3 2 1

For my wife, Christy,
whose patience, wisdom, and kindness
help me sweep the webs
of sin from my life

CONTENTS

1

THE TANGLED WEB
INIQUITY WEAVES

The cursed earth is not so apt to be overgrown with weeds, briers, and thorns, as this soul of mine with lusts, passions, distempers, worldly cares, and sinful thoughts, the law of the flesh rebelleth against the law of my mind, and diffuseth its venom into every action I perform, and carrieth me violently to the committing of sin against knowledge and conscience.[1]

We pause, eyeing the blackness uneasily. Musty air creeps out. The darkness stops us. That darkness wouldn't concern us so much, if it didn't conspire to hide other dangers. If there were no pits, no sharp corners, no startling noises, and no webs—the truth comes out—no webs to entangle us in their sudden, resilient stickiness. No webs to snatch at our faces. No webs to stretch out their invisible, tensile fingers until they drive us back sputtering. Few people enjoy venturing into the dark recesses of a basement or down a dimly lit trail without a strong flashlight to expose the nets strung across their path.

Because they are so visceral, we react to spider webs more than we do to less tangible dangers. We recoil at a web, for instance, but become quite comfortable with our sinful tendencies and their devastating consequences. We hire exterminators to crawl in, around, and under our houses in the quest to destroy tiny

---

[1] Robert Bolton, *The Carnal Professor: Discovering the Woeful Slavery of a Man Guided by the Flesh* (1634; repr., Ligonier, PA: Soli Deo Gloria, 1992), 19.

adversaries, while we incautiously dismiss "small sins" as insignificant. We hide or dismiss our little vices rather than eradicate them. We use brooms to sweep out webs, keeping them at arm's length, while we incautiously brush up against sin and are snared in it. We choose a circuitous route to avoid an area filled with webs, while we walk right into habitual sins with hardly a thought. We are inconsistent creatures—judging non-threats to be serious and deadly poisons to be harmless.

Sin is a snare. We learned as children that temptation is a snare that can drag us into sin, but the sin that follows temptation is a snare in itself. Individual sins are strands in a web of vice that slowly traps and destroys its victims. Solomon says, "By transgression an evil man is ensnared, but the righteous sings and rejoices" (Prov. 29:6, NASB).

WHO CARES AND WHY DOES IT MATTER?

Everyone can profit from a thoughtful exposé of vice, but I have a special concern for two groups.[2] First, high-school and college-age Christians are learning and building spiritual disciplines (as well as their dispositions toward evil) that will last a lifetime. The spiritual decisions made at this age will affect the course of life. Many young people will "depart from iniquity" (2 Tim. 2:19) in a fashion so decisive that though they continue to struggle against sin, they remain committed, godly believers whose lives are a tribute to God's grace. Others determine at this stage of life that sin poses little threat to them. They accept the philosophy of the flesh,

---

[2] Understanding the scope of a book helps us have appropriate expectations of it. This book does not deal with temptation (its origin or processes), original sin, or the physical consequences of sin. It also will not explore all the biblical terms for sin or for particular sins. The reader should not anticipate a systematic theology of sin. Instead it addresses sin as an entrapping web and specific instances of sin as strands in that web. As we become more aware of what a trap looks like, we will avoid it more readily.

thinking that parents and preachers have exaggerated the negative effects of sin and have concealed the exhilarating aspects of sin. These young people will reject counsel concerning the world and the flesh and walk boldly into petty sins that, while manageable for a time, will soon harden into established vices.

Second, I have great concern for servants of God whose lives are routinely wrecked and ruined by Satan's snares. Of all people, the servants of God should not be "ignorant of his devices" (2 Cor. 2:11), yet they falter, often catastrophically, in the long course of life and ministry. There's no simplistic solution to this problem. Sin infiltrates our lives as readily as cobwebs fill the corners of our houses. We sweep them out only to see them return unbidden, unannounced, and as numerous as before. The servant of God spends so much time sweeping sin out of other lives that he may neglect his own, and the little sins that set the course of our character begin to pile up. Sin breeds sin. So the failure to eradicate the entire web of sin in our lives leaves tattered strands of evil that are easily spun again. At this point, we become even more culpable for our failure since "this is not the fall of one who is *overtaken* in a fault; but of one who is entangled in the net of his own corruptions. One sin prepares the way for another. Like the insect enfolded in the spider's web, he loses all power of resistance, and falls a prey to the destroyer."[3]

> *Because they are so visceral, we react to spider webs more than we do to less tangible dangers . . . judging non-threats to be serious and deadly poisons to be harmless.*

---

[3] Andrew Fuller, *The Backslider: His Nature, Symptoms, and Means for Recovery* (1801; repr., Birmingham: Solid Ground Christian Books, 2005), 23–24.

We become better equipped to handle sin in our lives when we follow a procedure that arms us with knowledge and exposes sin with light. Knowledge tells us ahead of time where we're likely to find traps of sin, what they look like, and how to avoid them. God's Word shines a light into the recesses of our hearts to reveal what's already going on inside of us. Our natural tendency toward self-justification resists such exposure; so unless we're committed to a sustained campaign against sin, we will treat our sin far too lightly and will fail to expose its hold on our hearts.

Sometimes we recognize the wrong that we've done and repent of it only to see a greater variety of sins crowd in to take its place. While this situation may have several causes, I'm concerned that we sometimes carefully snip out portions of the web of sin while leaving the main radials of that web intact. We then either feign or experience real astonishment when the web is rebuilt in short order. Understanding the interconnectedness of sins may help us diagnose and destroy the underlying causes of our sin more effectively.

A spider web has three components that are relevant to our discussion. The *frame* constitutes the superstructure on which the rest of the web hangs. It's analogous to our fallen creatureliness—that without which no web of vice could be built in our lives. The *radials* are the "spokes" that connect the frame to the center. In terms of our study, these radials represent the capital sins—sins of the heart that give structure to the individual acts of sin that we commit. The *spirals* are the nearly circular structures that coil outward from the center. These spirals are the sticky parts of the web that catch insects. They're analogous to individual, recognizable acts of sin.

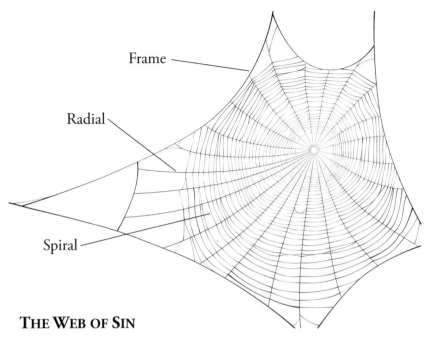

Frame

Radial

Spiral

THE WEB OF SIN

The idea of sin as a web originates from the Bible's depiction of individuals whose sin leads to other sins. This interrelation of sins occurs so frequently and extensively that it seems impossible to commit a single sin as an isolated act. Sin is nearly always a complex, interlocking web in which motives, roots, manifestations, and resultant sins all tangle together.[4]

Building an argument on an analogy can be dangerous. Our fertile imaginations can visualize connections that don't exist. We can press images too far (can anyone identify the type of spider or articulate the chemistry of the web-fibers?). But we often think in

---

[4] While other writers have recognized the interconnectedness of sin, none, to my knowledge, have devoted full attention to the complexity of the problem. John Cassian, for example, argues that "gluttony, fornication, covetousness, anger, dejection, [sloth] have a sort of connexion with each other, and are, so to speak, linked together in a chain, so that any excess of the one forms a starting point for the next" (John Cassian, *Conferences* V.10), but Cassian links these sins only in the order given above. He puts sloth at the end of the chain, but the situation is vastly more complex than he represents. Sloth can cause or result from any of the other sins. Lust may stem from envy or cause envy and so on.

images. Treating sin as a web concretizes important biblical truths that may help us respond properly to sin.

Sin Is Often Inadvertent

The fly goes about his own business with no suspicion that his entire life is about to be ended. He never intended to fall into a life-terminating snare. He didn't even know the spider's web was there. But his ignorance makes no difference to the spider. Pleading ignorance does not avert the consequences although it may make a person less culpable than he might have otherwise been. Here we face the first characteristic of a web. It traps those who are oblivious just as readily as it ensnares those who sin deliberately.

The book of Proverbs warns the insensible, but it doesn't revoke the consequences for the sin committed in ignorance. "[I] beheld among the simple ones, I discerned among the youths, a young man void of understanding, passing through the street near her corner; and he went the way to her house. . . . He goeth after her straightway, as an ox goeth to the slaughter, or as a fool to the correction of the stocks; till a dart strike through his liver; as a bird hasteth to the snare, and knoweth not that it is for his life" (Prov. 7:7–8, 22–23). The fact that there are serious natural consequences for sin ought to make the people of God more alert to it in their own lives. The Bible doesn't encourage a flippant, careless attitude toward sin.[5] While it's true that God forgives, that His grace abounds more than our sin, and that the eternal death our

---

[5] For example Tina Chan boasts that sin is constructive in "Review of Simon Laham, *The Science of Sin: The Psychology of the Seven Deadlies (and Why They Are So Good for You)," Library Journal* 137, no. 2 (Feb. 2012): 79–80. The imperatives of the New Testament establish a God-ordained means of sanctification that does not have a cavalier attitude toward sin. We ought to appreciate Titus 2:11 and 2:12, "For the grace of God that bringeth salvation hath appeared to all men, teaching us that, denying ungodliness and worldly lusts, we should live soberly, righteously, and godly, in this present world."

sin deserves has been done away in Christ, these truths don't mean that sin has minimal to no consequence for the believer. Only the grace of God exhibited through the death of Jesus Christ can free us from our sin—our feeble attempts to cut through the web of vice in our own strength are futile.

But enough evidence exists in the New Testament epistles to conclude that Christians can and do experience serious consequences for their sin. It's hard to resist the force of Paul's words: "For he that eateth and drinketh unworthily, eateth and drinketh damnation to himself, not discerning the Lord's body. For this cause many are weak and sickly among you, and many sleep. For if we would judge ourselves, we should not be judged. But when we are judged, we are chastened of the Lord" (1 Cor. 11:29–32). From the temporary delivering over of someone "unto Satan for the destruction of the flesh" (5:5) to the permanent loss of eternal rewards (3:15), consequences for sin apply to the believer. In other words, the Bible leads us to conclude that sin really does trap and destroy believers in its complex web.

> *Many small sins seem trivial. They occur in the heart. No one sees them. No one knows. No one seems to get hurt. But don't mistake invisibility for insignificance.*

And there's another important truth related to the inadvertency of sin. The person who stumbles into sin isn't as culpable as the one who sins knowingly and willfully. We shouldn't treat every sinner alike. When we treat every sin as if it were deliberate and high-handed, dealing out wrath in judgment without mercy, we're ignoring God's plea for His people to "restore such an one in the spirit of meekness" (Gal. 6:1).[6] A web is a snare. We don't have to be looking for trouble to get caught in it.

Since sin is this terrible web that catches us when we're heedless, we must know what is good and true and distinguish it from everything false and evil. "A prudent man foreseeth the evil, and hideth himself: but the simple pass on, and are punished" (Prov. 22:3). We must guard our thinking and behavior preemptively. Some thoughts lead to very dark places. "But they that will be rich fall into temptation and a snare, and into many foolish and hurtful lusts, which drown men in destruction and perdition" (1 Tim. 6:9). Those who do not consciously avoid sin will stumble into it unexpectedly. Their unwillingness isn't an adequate defense. Because of the inadvertent nature of some sin, one of our first steps in avoiding its web is acquiring wisdom.

Sin Seems Inconsequential

Spider webs are unpleasant but not especially life threatening to us. In fact, even when we notice them, they're so thin and wispy that they seem utterly inconsequential. But if we walk through one, it suddenly becomes significant to us. A web doesn't look like much, but its tensile strength is phenomenal. Many scientific studies have shown that spider silk is stronger and more capable of bending without breaking than steel of the same weight. It is highly effective for its purposes.

---

[6] See also James 5:19–20, "Brethren, if any of you do err from the truth, and one convert him; let him know, that he which converteth the sinner from the error of his way shall save a soul from death, and shall hide a multitude of sins." In this context, *convert* cannot refer to conversion to spiritual salvation. The phrase "if any of you" occurs several other times in James and always refers to believers. In this context the one who is straying from the truth is a fellow believer.

Many small sins seem trivial. They occur in the heart. No one sees them. No one knows. No one seems to get hurt. But don't mistake invisibility for insignificance. Obvious webs don't catch the fly. The well-spun web ensnares because of its inconspicuousness and strength. This fact led Robert Bolton to conclude, "The less discernible vice is, the greater care we should have to avoid it."[7] In keeping with the insidiousness of webs, moral snares seem light and trivial to us upon observation, but they're entangling upon contact.

Sin snares our minds by keeping us from grasping the seriousness of sin, by keeping us from appreciating grace, and by keeping us from a proper submission to God. Those who minimize sin do us no favors, and those who indiscriminately assert that the ministers of God who draw attention to sin's hideousness are legalists are themselves ignoring Scripture. They deaden us to sin's threat. Such voices comfort us by saying that a casual stroll down sin's dark corridors will be no threat to God's grace. They are either ignorant of the snares stretched across the path or have gotten themselves too thoroughly entangled to notice or care. The Greek New Testament contains over sixteen hundred imperatives, and a significant number of them are commands concerning sin.[8] Far from treating sin lightly, the Bible gives some startling expressions of sin's seriousness:

Pride or vanity
> Take heed that ye do not your alms before men, to be seen of them: otherwise ye have no reward of your Father which is in heaven. (Matt. 6:1)

---

[7] Bolton, *The Carnal Professor*, 74.

[8] Including the hortatory subjunctives and prohibitory subjunctives would increase the number of commands significantly.

Greed

Lay not up for yourselves treasures upon earth, where moth and rust doth corrupt, and where thieves break through and steal. (Matt. 6:19)

Anger

Dearly beloved, avenge not yourselves, but rather give place unto wrath: for it is written, Vengeance is mine; I will repay, saith the Lord. (Rom. 12:19)

Lust

Flee fornication. Every sin that a man doeth is without the body; but he that committeth fornication sinneth against his own body. (1 Cor. 6:18)

Lust, greed, and gluttony

Know ye not that the unrighteous shall not inherit the kingdom of God? Be not deceived: neither fornicators, nor idolaters, nor adulterers, nor effeminate, nor abusers of themselves with mankind, nor thieves, nor covetous, nor drunkards, nor revilers, nor extortioners, shall inherit the kingdom of God. (1 Cor. 6:9–10)

Envy

But if ye have bitter envying and strife in your hearts, glory not, and lie not against the truth. (James 3:14)

Sloth

For even when we were with you, this we commanded you, that if any would not work, neither should he eat. For we hear that there are some which walk among you disorderly, working not at all, but are busybodies. Now them that are such we command and exhort by our Lord Jesus Christ, that with quietness they work, and eat their own bread. (2 Thess. 3:10–12)

Sin in general

If thy right eye offend thee, pluck it out, and cast it from thee: for it is profitable for thee that one of thy members should perish, and not that thy whole body should be cast into hell. And if thy right hand offend thee, cut it off, and cast it from thee: for it is profitable for thee that one of thy members should perish, and not that thy whole body should be cast into hell. (Matt. 5:29–30)

Certain sins might seem negligible in their effect, but all sin is part of a great web of sin that slowly captures and ruins lives. Minimizing sin and its consequences is a swift means of trapping and destroying the incautious mind and heart.

Sin Is Individual

I once watched a fly struggle in a single strand of a spider's web. A part of me rooted for the spider in its relentless extermination of such "undesirables," but another part wanted victory for the captive. When it first hit the web, only two feet of the fly were bound, but as it struggled to free itself, it thrashed violently from side to side, gradually trapping its other feet and finally its wings in the surrounding threads. I shouted, "Stop flinging yourself around wildly and focus on the thread that has caught you!" Alas, he spoke no English. And I speak no Fly.

We tend to get caught in one thread of a web before we're ensnared in others. This holds true in the natural world and the spiritual world. While sins are ultimately interconnected, they're also individual. If we don't recognize what specific threads are snaring us at a given moment, we'll flounder into greater entrapment as additional threads get wrapped around us, binding us with greater strength.

This brings urgency to our spiritual analysis. We may be struggling with only one or a few sins at the moment, but if we don't escape them, they will become not only more frequent and powerful individually but also corporately. The close examination of our spiritual life must be both extensive (seeing what sins are connected to each other) and intensive (seeing what sins are immediately present).

A web traps those who are oblivious just as readily as it ensnares those who sin deliberately.

Sin Is Interconnected

There are many types of spider webs—from the neatly circular garden-variety web spiraling outward on well-defined radials to the confusing jumble of silk in a tangle web or sheet web. But a web is never a single one-directional strand. Likewise, sin is a complex of interconnected motives, thoughts, and actions. In the subsequent chapters we'll explore the thesis that there's never a solitary sin. Like the silk of a spider web, sin connects with sin. There are central sins that lead to radial (outlying) sins. There are outlying sins that cause or at least foster additional radial sins. But sin loves company, especially the company of other sins.

The Bible presents a brief taxonomy of sin when it reduces "all that is in the world" to the three categories of "the lust of the flesh, and the lust of the eyes, and the pride of life" (1 John 2:16). It seems likely that these three describe the root motives from which all sin springs. We want to feel physical, sensory things. We want to have (to acquire and possess) things. We want to be great and experience greatness. In the desire to diagnose sin correctly, many early church fathers started with this biblical taxonomy and worked toward other root thoughts that stimulated specific sinful actions. This leads us to consider what the church has traditionally called the capital sins.

THE SEVEN CAPITAL SINS

The Bible implies the existence of foundational sins. We cannot read Paul's warning that "the love of money is the root of all evil" (1 Tim. 6:10) without admitting the capacity of certain sins to cause others. Several early church fathers, prior to the rise of the Roman Catholic Church, categorized sins, and sin lists began to identify those sins from which others sprang. Initially these were called capital sins—sins that served as the head of others.

The Roman Church took this biblical concept and corrupted it in later years, turning it into the "seven deadly sins," asserting that there were certain sins of such a heinous nature that they could separate a person from eternal life if that person died in an unrepentant state.[9] We utterly reject Catholic theology and its abuse of the biblical data. But we cannot reject the biblical data! The early church fathers referenced in this book antedated the Roman Catholic Church. I use them only insofar as their ideas reflect or corroborate Scripture. The Word of God, not human tradition, is our authority for faith and practice.

---

[9] For a summary of various interpretations, see Sam Storms, "Can a Christian Commit the Sin unto Death? A Study on 1 John 5:16–17," April 18, 2006, http://www.samstorms.com /all-articles/post/can-a-christian-commit-the-sin-unto-death---a-study-on-1-john-5:16-17.

A fourth-century church father, Evagrius (345–399), sifted through the sins listed in Scripture and identified eight evil thoughts that he believed to be the source of all other sins.[10] According to Evagrius, these eight evil thoughts originate in the heart before they breed specific external sins.[11] In the years following Evagrius, John Cassian (360–435) and others composed similar lists.[12] These lists were recombined by Gregory the Great (540–604)[13] as the seven capital sins—envy, gluttony, greed, lust, pride, sloth, and wrath (Table 1.1).[14] The Roman Catholic Church continued to view these seven capital vices as thought-oriented sins or sins of the heart and mind. In light of this fact, William Backus observes that none of the seven deadly sins is "a single, separate sinful behavior—not one is an individual action, such as killing or stealing. Instead, all of them are what

---

[10] Evagrius lived among the "desert fathers" as a monk after abandoning Constantinople due to the worldliness that it called out in his own life. Since he followed some of Origen's ideas, Evagrius was not among the most orthodox of the early Christian fathers. He is useful to us only for his accurate identification of sins that appear in Scripture.

[11] Evagrius believed that these eight evil thoughts stemmed from the underlying "thought" of self-love. His list in Greek is γαστριμαργία (*gastrimargia*), φιλαργυρία (*philargyria*), πορνεία (*porneia*), ὑπερηφανία (*hyperēphania*), λύπη (*lypē*), ἀκηδία (*akēdia*), κενοδοξία (*kenodoxia*), and ὀργή (*orgē*).

[12] John Cassian is best known for bringing Egyptian monasticism to Europe. Although his writings depicting orthodox Christology served as a defense against Nestorianism, some of his other beliefs were problematic. For example, he held to a position on salvation that came to be known as semi-Pelagianism, which teaches that the human will is active apart from the grace of God in choosing salvation. I don't hold him up as a model to be followed in doctrine, but he did recognize that certain sins give rise to others.

[13] A bishop of Rome who rejected the title of pope (though the later Roman Church called him a pope), Gregory the Great's monastic background influenced his attitudes toward sin and worship. Although we cannot concur with many of his beliefs, we recognize that unlike the popes who followed him, he was personally moral. In fact, John Calvin considered Gregory to be the last good pope (*Institutes of the Christian Religion*, Book IV.7).

[14] *Capital* simply indicates that these sins served as the "head" or source of the other specific sins. These were later called the seven deadly sins.

psychologists refer to as traits."[15] Backus is noting what others had observed before him—these seven sins are really vices, or established internal evil dispositions.

TABLE 1.1: HISTORICAL IDENTIFICATIONS OF SOURCE SINS

	Evagrius	Cassian	Gregory I
envy (*invidia*)			•
fornication (*fornicatio*)		•	
gluttony (*gula*)	•	•	•
greed (*avaritia*)	•	•	•
lust (*luxuria*)	•		•
pride (*superbia*)	•	•	•
sadness (*tristitia*)	•	•	
sloth (*acedia*)	•	•	•
vainglory (*vanagloria*)	•	•	
wrath (*ira*)	•	•	•

In the years following Gregory, other theologians began arranging specific sins under the vice that they considered most likely to be their root cause.[16] For example, one biblical sin list provides subsets to the capital vice of wrath:

---

[15] William Backus, *What Your Counselor Never Told You: Seven Secrets Revealed—Conquer the Power of Sin in Your Life* (Minneapolis: Bethany House, 2000), 39.

[16] See for instance Marion Le Roy Burton, *The Problem of Evil: A Criticism of the Augustinian Point of View* (Chicago: Open Court Publishing Company, 1909), 157. "It would be useless to enumerate the various acts and states which are described as sins, but it is a significant fact that out from this heterogeneous mass of evil acts, certain sins emerge which may be regarded as typical and as including all the lesser sins."

> Let all bitterness, and wrath, and anger, and clamour, and
> evil speaking, be put away from you, with all malice. (Eph.
> 4:31)

And another touches the root vices of wrath, pride, and lust:

> For I fear that perhaps when I come I may find you not as I
> wish, and that you may find me not as you wish—that per-
> haps there may be quarreling, jealousy, anger, hostility, slan-
> der, gossip, conceit, and disorder. I fear that when I come
> again my God may humble me before you, and I may have
> to mourn over many of those who sinned earlier and have
> not repented of the impurity, sexual immorality, and sensu-
> ality that they have practiced. (2 Cor. 12:20–21, ESV)

As Christians have studied Scripture and analyzed the practical
evidence all around them in life, many have realized that sins are
interwoven. So, while the choice of imagery is my own, the use
of a web as our primary analogy fits what we have long known to
be true about sin. If we understand that web, we will understand
ourselves more fully. And if we understand that web, we might cut
its threads more swiftly as they appear in our lives so that we don't
find ourselves trapped in a web of sin.

Different organizational patterns treat these seven capital sins. All
sins abuse love (the failure to love God with all our heart and to
love our neighbor as ourselves, Matt. 22:37–39), but not all sins
distort love in the same way. This has led some writers to separate
sins into categories of *cold* and *warm*. Cold sins lack love or exhibit only self-love. They're utterly defective because they fail to
love God and others at all and fail to love self appropriately. Warm
sins on the other hand exhibit love in an inappropriate fashion.

There may be some sort of love for God, others, and self, but it is corrupted love.[17] Additionally, there are material sins that pertain to the stuff of the world around us and immaterial sins that operate only in the spiritual realm. Table 1.2 illustrates the alignment of these sins with each other.

TABLE 1.2: ORGANIZATION OF THE SEVEN CAPITAL SINS

	Cold	Warm
Material	greed	gluttony, lust
Immaterial	envy, pride, sloth	anger

All the capital vices are serious due to their propensity to spawn numerous other sins. But given the four divisions above, which category seems the most serious? Theologians have typically recognized the most serious of the sins to be pride and envy and the least serious to be gluttony. The utter love-deficiency of the cold sins makes them the prime candidates for censure. But in practice, which of the sins does the church single out for the greatest condemnation? Lust! The theologian protests rightly that Jesus treated the slothful, prideful, and greedy with great severity (Matt. 23:4–12, 25–31) but the lustful with tender rebuke (Luke 7:36–50; John 4:4–29). But sad to say, Christ's followers haven't always agreed with their Master. We could use these observations to defend various forms of lust, but that would be missing the point entirely. Jesus treated the adulterous woman and the prostitute with holy tenderness. He didn't justify their sin or leave them in it. But His condemnation of the proud, envious Pharisee revealed that some sins really are more serious because they cut a person off from the grace of God.

---

[17] See Dorothy Sayers, *The Whimsical Christian* (New York: Macmillan, 1978), 159.

Conclusion

The following chapters treat the seven capital sins in an arrange-ment that moves from cold to warm sins. These seven vices are the moral equivalent to the radials inside the frame of a spider web. With Scripture as our guide, we will begin to see how individual sins connect with other sins.

2

Envy—Entangled
in Resentment

> Among the seven deadly sins, envy, I feel, may be the most pervasive, interpenetrating as it so insidiously does the other six major sins. . . . Envy, to qualify as envy, has to have a strong touch—sometimes more than a touch—of malice behind it. Malice that cannot speak its name, cold-blooded but secret hostility, impotent desire, hidden rancor, and spite all cluster at the center of envy.[1]

Each of the seven capital sins, with the exception of envy and sloth, is a corruption of something good.[2] But there's nothing positive about envy. It's the coldest of the cold sins. Like anger, envy seeks to destroy. Unlike anger, envy makes no pretense of seeking justice.

Defining Envy

Envy is an acute, sustained resentment of other people for possessing good things or for experiencing blessings that the envious person lacks coupled with a desire to see others deprived of that good. It typically manifests itself in one of two ways: grieving about the good that others experience or rejoicing over their misfortunes. Scott Sullender notes, "Envy leads to being chronically resentful of what others have and to complaining about how unfairly one has

---

[1] Joseph Epstein, *Envy: The Seven Deadly Sins* (Oxford: University Press, 2003), xvi, 7.

[2] The most comprehensive work on envy is Helmut Schoeck, *Envy: A Theory of Social Behavior*, trans. Michael Glenny and Betty Ross (New York: Harcourt, Brace & World, Inc., 1966).

been treated by God, others, or life itself."[3] The Old Testament uses a single word to express the twin concepts of jealousy and envy.[4] They are related in the zealousness of their passion. Jealousy arises when we're deprived of something that we feel rightly belongs to us (such as the affections of a spouse). Envy arises when someone else possesses what we lack. MacKay casts this well, "Envy is the child of hate: jealousy is the offspring of love. Envy is a sense of bitterness over what is not our own: jealousy is a feeling of wrong at being deprived of what we believe rightly or wrongly to be our own."[5] Envy is also related to greed—in greed we stretch out our hands to acquire what we think we lack, but in envy we stretch out our hands to destroy the person who possesses what we lack.

We don't have to be taught to envy others. When a classmate showed up at grade school with a new toy that our parents couldn't afford to buy us, we not only wanted it (greed) but also resented our classmate for having it (envy). Surely we deserve at least as much as everyone else has, we reason. It doesn't seem fair that God would give better things to others than to us. Our flesh conspires with Satan to increase the frequency and intensity of our resentment toward others and ultimately toward God for the perceived unfairness of our life situation. Modern societies proactively breed

Envy never actually benefits the envious person psychologically or materially. Greed acquires new possessions, and lust has its own thrills, but envy only destroys.

---

[3] Scott Sullender, "The Seven Deadly Sins as a Pastoral Diagnostic System," *Pastoral Psychology* 64 (2015): 220.

[4] Transliterated, this term is the noun *qin'ah* or the verb *qana'*.

[5] W. Mackintosh Mackay, *The Disease and Remedy of Sin* (London: Hodder and Stoughton, 1918), 80.

envy. Political parties cynically gain power by stirring up resentment against those who have more than we do.[6] They promise to redistribute wealth once they gain office. This behavior openly incites people to envy. In discussing welfare as the direct product of envy, Sayers notes: "The only difference [between charity and welfare] is this: that people will no longer pay because they want to—eagerly and for love—but because they must, reluctantly and under pain of fine or imprisonment. The result, roughly speaking, is financially the same; the only difference is the elimination of the two detested virtues of love and gratitude."[7] This observation is truly culturally damning. Our society has devoted itself to the eradication of genuine love and has steadily replaced that love with legislated envy.

Resentment arises when one star athlete makes twenty times what anyone else on the team makes. Bitterness pursues the starlet who was born into wealth, which she squanders. She possesses no life skills, no wisdom, no profound intellect, and achieves no lasting good that deserves such good fortune. It's not fair that we struggle to make ends meet while she lives a high life simply because she was born into wealth. Life seems to have dealt the envious person a bitter hand. Other people have nicer families, higher paying jobs, more opportunities, flashier vacations, stronger investments, greater popularity, better health, more friends, and bigger houses, and it's not fair.

---

[6] "There is a fatal socialism that merely wishes to pull a few people down, rather than pull a large number up; and although throughout its history it has seldom come fully to grips with the Envy that the leveling impulse will always too easily incite, socialism has seldom before been so generally mean-spirited and at the same time self-righteous in its claims." Henry Fairlie, *The Seven Deadly Sins Today* (Washington, DC: New Republic Books, 1978), 81.

[7] Sayers, *The Whimsical Christian*, 174–75.

Envy festers like a canker. It doesn't do anyone any good. Since the envious person rarely acquires the good thing that he resents in someone else, his envy gnaws away at contentment, civility, and kindness in his own heart without achieving any virtuous objective. The envier becomes Uriah Heep, the fawning, "'umble" schemer in Charles Dickens's *David Copperfield*, who plots the malicious overthrow of those who seem to have always had it easy. Heep gains nothing other than a temporary, intangible triumph of raw power over the objects of his envy. He ends up in prison, his envy and its connected crimes unmasked. One commentator says that Heep is "bent on the destruction of anyone and everyone who has it better . . . . The humiliation and degradation of [his lower-class status] has filled him with such rage against the whole world that he'll do whatever he can to ruin the lives of people in higher social classes."[8] Heep is one of Charles Dickens's most hateful characters, and that malevolence stems from his envy.

KEY SCRIPTURE PASSAGES ON ENVY

The Bible affirms the components of envy that we have seen above: (1) resentment (2) at the good possessed or experienced by others (3) that has been denied to oneself (4) coupled with the desire to destroy the person who has experienced that good. Solomon, for instance, mourns the fact that even when a man works hard to earn a wage or reward, other people despise him for possessing more than they have. "Again, I considered all travail, and every right work, that for this a man is envied of his neighbour. This is also vanity and vexation of spirit" (Eccles. 4:4). Notice the Philistines' reaction when Isaac moved near the coast of Canaan: "For he had possession of flocks, and possession of herds, and great store of servants: and the Philistines envied him. For all the wells which his

---

[8] "Uriah Heep," http://www.shmoop.com/david-copperfield/uriah-heep.html.

father's servants had digged in the days of Abraham his father, the Philistines had stopped them, and filled them with earth" (Gen. 26:14–15). The Philistines could have used the wells that Abraham had dug. They could have increased their own flocks through careful management of those wells. But they were so concerned about other people's prospering through the use of the wells that they filled them in. This verse reveals the irrational behavior spawned by envy—it so desperately wants to destroy someone else that it doesn't care if it destroys itself in the process.

Envy destroys family relationships by stirring up conflict, meanness, and even hatred between those who should love each other unconditionally. "And when Rachel saw that she bare Jacob no children, Rachel envied her sister; and said unto Jacob, Give me children, or else I die" (Gen. 30:1). "[Joseph's] brethren envied him" (Gen. 37:11), and "the patriarchs, moved with envy, sold Joseph into Egypt" (Acts 7:9). Envy corrupts the minds of people so that they refuse to follow God's appointed leaders anymore. They want the authority and power that God has ordained for others, but they cannot have it. So they resist. The inspired commentary on the rebellion of Dathan and Abiram links their revolt to envy: "They envied Moses also in the camp, and Aaron the saint of the Lord. The earth opened and swallowed up Dathan, and covered the company of Abiram" (Ps. 106:16–17).

Envy can drive spiritual leaders to compete against each other. In at least one instance in the New Testament, certain Christian evangelists sought to harm Paul emotionally by stealing his "market share" of the church while Paul was in prison. "Some indeed preach Christ even of envy and strife; and some also of good will: the one preach Christ of contention, not sincerely, supposing to add affliction to my bonds" (Phil. 1:15–16). This passage indicates that envy can actually spur ministry activity even while robbing the envious person of any reward that his ministry might have gained. We can maintain a guise of being zealous for the truth when in reality the accolades given to others rankle us deeply.

Envy is often invisible to the envious person but obvious to the onlooker. If you could have asked the chief priests, Sadducees, and Pharisees why they put Jesus Christ on trial and had Him crucified, they would have come up with a number of reasons. He was a threat to the political order, and that could cost the lives of thousands of Jews if Rome had to intervene to suppress a revolt (John 11:49–50). He violated the Sabbath (they actually tried to pin this one on Him, but they couldn't find adequate testimony to prove any violation). They said He was a blasphemer (Matt. 26:63–66), but they arrested Jesus before they had any evidence against Him (Matt. 26:59). That's not the behavior of a legitimate court in the pursuit of justice. When they brought Jesus to Pilate, the governor saw through their trumped-up charges to the real motive for their behavior. "[Pilate] knew that for envy they had delivered him" (Matt. 27:18, cf. Mark 15:10). Jesus exhibited a power, wisdom, and goodness that the spiritual leaders of His day did not. He held the hearts of the people. He healed the sick and forgave sinners. The spiritual leaders hated Jesus for His goodness, not for any evil that they could identify in Him.[9] Their evil disposition displays the insidiousness of envy. It creeps around

> *Envy is often invisible to the envious person but obvious to the onlooker.*

---

[9] When Jesus asked His spiritual adversaries, "Which one of you convicts me of sin?" (John 8:46, ESV), no one volunteered a response. At that point in Christ's ministry, the spiritual leaders of Judea already hated and envied Him, and they had made abortive attempts to get rid of Him, but they had not articulated or attempted a coherent plan to destroy Him.

in the shadows setting traps, slinging an occasional stone, plotting malice, and waiting for an opportunity to cause the utter downfall of the person envied.

Envy never actually benefits the envious person psychologically or materially. Greed acquires new possessions, and lust has its own thrills, but envy only destroys. And it needs no cause other than its own wounded pride to seek the ruin of others. As an envious person unable to abide the superiority of others, you want the whole world torn down (as does Satan), even to your own detriment, so that all are inferior to yourself.

INTERCONNECTIONS WITH OTHER SINS

Envy doesn't keep good company. In several significant passages, it appears alongside the worst of human sins. These passages unmask envy for what it really is. Envy is not a trifling, closeted sin with little effect on the people of God. It's mature malice. It's nurtured hate. It's long-cherished malevolence. Scripture discloses these friends of envy:

> . . . being filled with all unrighteousness, fornication, wickedness, covetousness, maliciousness; full of envy, murder, debate, deceit, malignity; whisperers, backbiters, haters of God, despiteful, proud, boasters, inventors of evil things, disobedient to parents, without understanding, covenantbreakers, without natural affection, implacable, unmerciful: who knowing the judgment of God, that they which commit such things are worthy of death, not only do the same, but have pleasure in them that do them. (Rom. 1:29–32)

Now the works of the flesh are manifest, which are these; Adultery, fornication, uncleanness, lasciviousness, idolatry, witchcraft, hatred, variance, emulations, wrath, strife, seditions, heresies, envyings, murders, drunkenness, revellings, and such like: of the which I tell you before, as I have also told you in time past, that they which do such things shall not inherit the kingdom of God. (Gal. 5:19–21)

He is proud, knowing nothing, but doting about questions and strifes of words, whereof cometh envy, strife, railings, evil surmisings, perverse disputings of men of corrupt minds, and destitute of the truth, supposing that gain is godliness: from such withdraw thyself. (1 Tim. 6:4–5)

For we ourselves also were sometimes foolish, disobedient, deceived, serving divers lusts and pleasures, living in malice and envy, hateful, and hating one another. (Titus 3:3)

Wherefore laying aside all malice, and all guile, and hypocrisies, and envies, and all evil speakings . . . (1 Pet. 2:1)

Other sources concur with this biblical assessment. Lance Webb observes, "Envy is self-love unable to permit anyone to excel or rise above one's own superiority, with resulting hate, jealousy, intolerance, prejudice, slander, gossip, and the use of sarcasm or more violent means of leveling others to one's own height."[10] Robert McCracken notes, "Envy exacts a heavy toll. It makes its victim petulant, jealous, spiteful, mean."[11] To envy is to succumb to a vast web of sins that ensnare and destroy one's peace, love, and joy.

---

[10] Lance Webb, *Conquering the Seven Deadly Sins* (Nashville: Abingdon, 1955), 41.

[11] Robert J. McCracken, *What Is Sin? What Is Virtue?* (New York: Harper & Row, 1966), 19.

Sources of Envy

There's more to be told of the tale of envy. It not only keeps bad company, but it also results from other sins and causes other sins. While sin needs no other cause than the corruption of our fallen nature, we're sometimes shocked at the swiftness of its ascendency and the strength of its grip on us. It's like a spider's web that materializes overnight and can trap hundreds of insects in its time. Envy rarely "comes out of nowhere," and it never sits idly in the heart without plotting additional mischief.

We might ask why the primary examples of envy in Scripture (Joseph's brothers and the spiritual leaders at the time of Christ) nursed such malevolence against people who had done them no wrong. The question is simultaneously fair and yet misguided. The envious person *does* feel himself to be wronged, but he feels that he has incurred that wrong from the hand of God (or fate, fortune, or luck for the one who rejects God). He feels keenly the sting of deprivation even though the person who has experienced blessing may not have actively deprived the envious of anything. Joseph did not steal his father's affection, nor did he conspire with God to gain supremacy over his brothers. He simply had his father's special love, and he dreamed what God had chosen to reveal. His brothers could evaluate thus: "We're just as smart as Joseph; we're from the same father; we grew up in the same household; we have the same spiritual heritage; it's not fair for Joseph to have such advantages." Likewise, Jesus Christ lived a humble, good, and constructive life, yet the spiritual leaders of Israel hated Him. Why? Because they felt their self-appointed authority challenged by Jesus' inherent authority. They felt their "market share" of the praise of the people diminishing. They couldn't stomach the fact that God had apparently given this untrained, backwater son-of-a-carpenter wisdom and power that they lacked. The Pharisees had guarded God's law for several centuries. They lived righteous lives by their standards. They taught the people. And yet God passed over them in His blessing. It wasn't fair!

If we are to understand envy, we have to understand that it's a petulant raging against God (or fate) for the inequitable distribution of good. What gives rise to such thinking? We never find envy without also unearthing pride. If we held God's perspective concerning ourselves—rightly appraising our being and responsibilities—we couldn't become envious. But it's often not enough to accept the good that God has given us without lamenting the appearance of greater good that He has given to someone else. If no one else possessed better things than we possess, we would be content; so our discontent springs from the fact that we think we deserve at least as good as anyone else in our situation. But this involves pride. First, we think that we have the right to define what is good. We think that we have the wisdom to discern all of the outworking of providence. Second, we think that we have the right to possess as much power, glory, wealth, fame, comfort, security—in a word, blessings—as anyone else possesses. Without pride, envy would wither away.

Greed can produce envy. By itself, greed simply wants to acquire more, but a person who starts with the motivation of acquiring more can spiral reflexively inward when someone else strikes it rich, hits the big one, or sees some investment soar unexpectedly. We consider our own investments at least as shrewd as his, but fate has intervened to propel him to the stratosphere of success while we languish in the plodding, paltry acquisitions so typical of investing.

Lust provokes envy. Desiring the beauty or relationship that someone else has, we can envy that beauty and wish to see it destroyed, or we can envy the relationship and wish to see it broken. Once we have seen beauty and attractiveness and want it for ourselves, in the darkness of our minds we reason that it's not fair for someone else to be married to such an attractive, successful, talented person. And we begin to resent others for the beauty and relationships that God has given to them.

Spawn of Envy

If envy serves as one of the main radials of the web of sin, it also gives rise to many spirals of evil. Rick Ezell notes, "Envy causes conflict with others, travels with its cousin anger, leads to depression, manifests itself in gossip, and can even pull the trigger on murder."[12]

When we resent someone else for the good that he possesses or experiences, every conceivable malicious response flows out of us. Look at the example of Joseph again. When his brothers envied him, they unleashed an avalanche of further evils. In Genesis 37, at least eleven additional sins attend the envy of Joseph's brothers. Table 2.1 depicts this series of interconnected evils. The fact that the brothers didn't actively go through with Joseph's murder doesn't make them less guilty of sin. Only Reuben's intervention delivered Joseph in the short term, and the presumption of a short and miserable life attended Joseph's sale into slavery. Look at how much evil stemmed from the envy of these men.

---

[12] Rick Ezell, *The Seven Sins of Highly Defective People* (Grand Rapids: Kregel, 2003), 37.

TABLE 2.1: SINS CONNECTED WITH ENVY—THE LIFE OF JOSEPH

Genesis	Verse	Sin
37:4	They hated him.	hatred
37:5	They hated him yet the more.	
37:8	They hated him yet the more [for his dreams and for his words].	
37:4	[They] could not speak peaceably unto him.	strife
37:18	They conspired against him to slay him.	murder, desecration
37:20	Come now therefore, and let us slay him, and cast him into some pit.	
37:20	We will say, Some evil beast hath devoured him.	lying, deception
37:31	They took Joseph's coat, and killed a kid of goats, and dipped the coat in the blood.	
37:20	We shall see what will become of his dreams.	mockery
37:23	They stript Joseph out of his coat, his coat of many colours that was on him.	theft
37:24	They took him, and cast him into a pit.	meanness, assault
37:27	Let us sell him to the Ishmeelites.	kidnapping, profiteering
37:28	[They] sold Joseph to the Ishmeelites for twenty pieces of silver.	
37:27	His brethren were content.	approval of evil
37:34	Jacob rent his clothes, and put sackcloth upon his loins, and mourned for his son many days.	cruel indifference
37:35	I will go down into the grave unto my son mourning. Thus his father wept for him.	

The most irrational, yet understandable, instance of envy in the history of the world occurred in the hostility of the Jewish spiritual leaders toward Christ. It was irrational because there was literally no wrongdoing in any of Jesus' actions nor in His heart. But this rejection was completely understandable because envy is always irrational, and who could be the better victim of wicked irrationality than the Son of God? Satan directed the fullness of his malice—the combining of his pride, his anger, his envy—at Jesus Christ; so it shouldn't surprise us that Satan's followers would do the same. Table 2.2 illustrates some of the passages that connect other sins to the envious thinking of the religious leaders. When they permitted envy in their hearts, they lost any semblance of righteousness and plunged into many evils—caught in a web of iniquity.

TABLE 2.2: SINS CONNECTED WITH ENVY—THE LIFE OF CHRIST

Matthew	Verse	Sin
9:26, 34	And the fame hereof went abroad into all that land. . . . But the Pharisees said, He casteth out devils through the prince of the devils.	slander
12:23–24	And all the people were amazed, and said, Is not this the son of David? But when the Pharisees heard it, they said, This fellow doth not cast out devils, but by Beelzebub the prince of the devils.	slander
26:67	Then did they spit in his face, and buffeted him; and others smote him with the palms of their hands.	assault
26:68	Prophesy unto us, thou Christ, Who is he that smote thee?	mockery
27:4	[Judas said] I have sinned in that I have betrayed the innocent blood. And they said, What is that to us?	malicious injustice

Matthew	Verse	Sin
27:20	The chief priests and elders persuaded the multitude that they should ask Barabbas, and destroy Jesus.	solicitation to evil, murder
27:24	Pilate saw that he could prevail nothing, but that rather a tumult was made.	inciting riot

Scattered passages throughout the New Testament add a few more sins to the list of those sins that derive from envy. In particular, envy frequently produces strife as Table 2.3 demonstrates. The final passage in this table conveys the causal nature of envy. It can produce every kind of evil as its offspring.

TABLE 2.3: SINS CONNECTED WITH ENVY—OTHER SCRIPTURES

Reference	Verse	Sin
Acts 13:45	When the Jews saw the multitudes, they were filled with envy, and spake against those things which were spoken by Paul, contradicting and blaspheming.	contention, slander
Acts 17:5–8	But the Jews which believed not, moved with envy, took unto them certain lewd fellows of the baser sort, and gathered a company, and set all the city on an uproar, and assaulted the house of Jason, and sought to bring them out to the people. And when they found them not, they drew Jason and certain brethren unto the rulers of the city, crying, These that have turned the world upside down are come hither also; whom Jason hath received: and these all do contrary to the decrees of Caesar, saying that there is another king, one Jesus. And they troubled the people and the rulers of the city, when they heard these things.	inciting riot, assault, distortion, lying
1 Corinthians 3:3	For ye are yet carnal: for whereas there is among you envying, and strife, and divisions, are ye not carnal, and walk as men?	strife, division, carnality

Reference	Verse	Sin
James 3:14	But if ye have bitter envying and strife in your hearts, glory not, and lie not against the truth.	strife, lying
James 3:16	For where envying and strife is, there is confusion and every evil work.	strife, rioting, all types of evil

Many times envy cannot injure others directly; so it nurses its grudge and hopes that calamity will devastate the object of its resentment. But envy frequently breeds more active sins, and it will continue to gnaw away at its adversary with an implacable resentment until the adversary is utterly destroyed. This relentless, ruthless pursuit of another person leads toward murder. Sometimes the envious person actually effects the murder as in the case of the Jewish spiritual rulers in the time of Christ. Envy was also the chief factor in the first murder since Cain resented Abel for being the recipient of God's blessing (Gen. 4:1–15). Sometimes the envious person chooses conspiracies or proxies to carry out his murderous intent as in the case of Joseph's brothers. Sometimes this murderous behavior occurs through character assassination (Acts 13:45), emotional maiming (Phil. 1:15–16), or an incessant sapping of the vital energy of an adversary (wherever strife appears).

ENVY TODAY

While we might wish that envy were confined to another era, the inexplicable, persistent malice that spews from the blogs, tweets, and op-ed columns of some individuals derives from envy. Not all criticism stems from envy. We should exercise due diligence to evaluate ourselves carefully in light of Scripture when we face censure from another believer or from this world. We are sinners still, and when someone levels an accusation at us, we ought to weigh its truthfulness judiciously. Evil deserves reproof. But the unwarranted vendettas and the persistent attempts to dig up evil about other people or institutions provides evidence that envy has ensnared a person in a strong web of vice.

If we can't wait for a coworker to botch his part of the coding for a new software release so that we can get his job, we have succumbed to envy. If we're disgusted that a classmate or coworker was selected for an honor, award, or raise, the resentment of envy has taken hold. When we complain to God about the resources that He has given to that profligate while we can barely make ends meet, we teeter on the brink of envy. Envy can drive the pastor to create new programs in order to surpass the numerical attendance at some other church. Envy lies behind much

Envy hides in our lives. Everyone can admit a little bit of pride (and do so with pride!), but envy seems too hideous for us to admit.

crestfallenness of heart and face. Envy breeds disappointment when someone else has more friends than we do on our favorite social networking site. Envy scowls when a younger employee is promoted to management. It turns away, biting a quivering lip in displeasure, when someone else has better things or is better at anything. We are envious of another's beauty or of her amiability, envious of property, envious of prestige, and envious of success.

The envious heart is just the beginning of evils because envy dreams evil and plots the downfall of others. It whispers that a teacher isn't as godly as he seems. It brazenly invents tales of wrongdoing perpetrated by its adversary. Envy slanders, stabs, bites, and gnaws through clever barbs or denigrating comments. Envy qualifies every word of praise that it hears about others—"Yes, he got his project in on time, but that's because he was given the easiest portion of the job"; "Of course, he's a more popular preacher because he caters to what people want to hear"; "Sure, she got promoted to manager, but that's because she flaunts her beauty and flatters the vice president."

Envy insinuates without evidence—"I'm not saying that there was any wrongdoing on her part, but her rapid rise seems a lot like someone I once knew who threw herself at every executive in the company"; "He might have gotten lucky on that land purchase, but I know for a fact that his sister is friends with someone on the tax board who forecloses on land in this area"; "Technically, that company didn't do anything illegal, but it's been a tyrannical abuser of its employees for a long time." In each case, envy seeks a conviction based on innuendo, deceit, and outright lies. Rebecca DeYoung summarizes the far-reaching effects of envy:

> Envy can show itself in the following ways: feeling offended at the talents, successes, or good fortune of others; selfish or unnecessary rivalry and competition; pleasure at others' difficulties or distress; ill will; reading false motives into others' behavior; belittling others; false accusations; backbiting (saying something bad, even if true, behind another's back); slander (saying something bad, even if true, in the open about someone); initiation, collection, or retelling of gossip; arousing, fostering, or organizing antagonism against others; scorn of another's abilities or failures; teasing or bullying; ridicule of persons, institutions, or ideals; and prejudice against those we consider

inferior, who consider us inferior, or who seem to threaten our security or position.[13]

Envy hides in our lives. Everyone can admit a little bit of pride (and do so with pride!), but envy seems too hideous for us to admit. Heidi Schlumpf conducted a survey showing that when asked to select "which Deadly Sin they struggled with the most," respondents marked envy next to last in frequency, with only seven percent of the total.[14] These findings indicate that very few people believe they struggle with envy. If we don't recognize the traits that characterize envy as well as the long-term consequences that spring from it, we may find ourselves tangled in a web of iniquity. Our thoughts and dispositions connect with many strands of sin. We may keep our thoughts pent up for a time (they seem trivial, like the radials of a web), but we will awaken one day to find ourselves trapped in the radiating sins of the web that cannot be hidden any longer.

---

[13] Rebecca Konyndyk DeYoung, *Glittering Vices: A New Look at the Seven Deadly Sins and Their Remedies* (Grand Rapids: Brazos, 2009), 45–46.

[14] Heidi Schlumpf, "Who's Afraid of the Seven Deadly Sins?" *U.S. Catholic* 65, no. 2 (February 2000): 22–25.

3

PRIDE—A DISTORTED
VIEW OF SELF

> Essentially sin is the exaltation of self. It represents the
> utterly false and futile effort of the individual to realize
> his low desire, or his highest good, in complete inde-
> pendence of or opposition to his fellow man and the
> changeless, rational, and beneficent will of his Creator;
> that is selfishness; that is sin.[1]

Pride defines us in our fallen state. We are beset with pride, and
most of us know it. In the Schlump survey about the seven capital sins, 49 percent of respondents cited pride as their chief sin.[2]
When we appreciate the fact that the next closest sin in this particular poll was claimed by only 12 percent of the respondents, the
pervasiveness of pride becomes apparent.

This pervasiveness doesn't apply to the modern era alone. Even in
the time of Augustine, the church recognized that pride was a uni-
versal human sin. In fact, it seemed to be the main sin underlying all other sins. "Every one, says Augustine, has fallen by pride,
which is the beginning of all sin."[3] The early church fathers were
not alone in this assessment. "Much of the Western tradition has
regarded pride as the root of all the other vices; it's the archetypical

---

[1] Marion Le Roy Burton, *The Problem of Evil: A Criticism of the Augustinian Point of
View* (Chicago: Open Court Publishing Company, 1909), 182.

[2] Heidi Schlumpf, "Who's Afraid of the Seven Deadly Sins?" *U.S. Catholic* 65, no. 2
(February 2000): 22–25.

[3] Burton, 160. See also Robert J. McCracken, *What Is Sin? What Is Virtue?* (New York:
Harper & Row, 1966), 11–12.

sin, the sin of the devil."[4] And even in the egocentrism, individu-
alism, and selfishness of the modern era, Jerry Bridges expresses

Pride blinds us to reality concerning ourselves and the world around us.

a prevailing Christian sentiment: "When I talk about specific areas of acceptable sins, one comment I often hear is that pride is the root cause of all of them."[5] James Stalker heightens our sense of the seriousness of pride when he says, "To [Jesus] pride appeared to be the master-sin."[6] He treated the pride of the Pharisees with much greater severity than the im-morality of adulteresses or the theft of tax collectors. Pride seems to be everywhere. Its prevalence calls for careful evaluation by the people of God. This is especially true in light of the modern ten-dency to dismiss the offensiveness of pride. Surveys from the first part of the twenty-first century have demonstrated that in America, pride is not even viewed by the majority of respondents as a sin.[7] We've been taught to take pride in our country, our culture, our possessions, and our achievements. We've been encouraged to have more self-esteem, self-awareness, and self-confidence. Everywhere we turn we're told to have things our way. Understanding pride should help us recognize its wrongfulness and to repent of it when it commandeers our hearts.

---

[4] William S. Stafford, *Disordered Loves: Healing the Seven Deadly Sins* (Boston: Cowley Publications, 1994), 118.

[5] Jerry Bridges, *Respectable Sins: Confronting the Sins We Tolerate* (Colorado Springs: NavPress, 2007), 53. Bridges disagrees slightly with this assessment. He qualifies this opinion that others have offered by stating, "While I agree that pride does play a major role in the development and expression of our subtle sins, I believe there is another sin that is even more basic, more widespread, and more apt to be the root cause of our others sins. That is the sin of *ungodliness*, of which we are all guilty to some degree."

[6] James Stalker, *The Seven Deadly Sins* (New York: Dodd, Mead, & Co., 1901), 13–14.

[7] Douglas M. Stenstrom and Mathew Curtis, "Pride, Sloth/Lust/Gluttony, Envy, Greed/Wrath: Rating the Seven Deadly Sins," *Interdisciplinary Journal of Research on Religion* 8 (2012): 9. This is an excellent article that shows modern American perceptions of the capital sins. Our culture views only greed and wrath as demonstrably sinful.

Defining Pride

Writers generally agree in their assessment of the nature of pride. Pride evaluates self inaccurately. Backus concludes, "Pride, more than any other sin, tends to involve disordered thinking."[8] Stalker observes, "In pride . . . there is always an element of falsehood. It is a claim to merits which are not possessed; or, if we possess them at all, we deceive ourselves and attempt to deceive others as to the degree in which we possess them."[9] Sullender adds, "Pride meant [to the church fathers] an over-estimation of one's self, an inflated ego that blocks one from seeing one's own failings or limitations."[10] Several common threads appear in these writers. Pride seems to involve (1) wrong thinking (2) about self (3) in a fashion that ultimately exalts self beyond the proper sphere. So in simplest terms, pride is inaccurate thinking about ourselves that exalts self above a true assessment of what we are as creatures.

Fundamentally, pride involves falsehood. It overestimates the capacities of our creatureliness. It rejects our limitations of knowledge and power and tries to override these limitations with a false sense of knowing or a false authority. If pride thinks inaccurately, then it is untrue to reality. In essence, it's a lie. Although pride is a foundational sin, we cannot define it fully without recourse to its connection with other sins. In fact, pride cannot exist apart from the lie. Rightly ordered and true thinking has no pride. Humility knows its true self, including its limitations and purpose for existence. The distorted thinking that accompanies pride creates such severe problems that it frequently leads to serious psychological

---

[8] William Backus, *What Your Counselor Never Told You: Seven Secrets Revealed. Conquer the Power of Sin in Your Life* (Minneapolis: Bethany House, 2000), 57–58.

[9] Stalker, 5–6.

[10] Scott Sullender, "The Seven Deadly Sins as a Pastoral Diagnostic System," *Pastoral Psychology* 64 (2015): 220.

consequences. William Backus connects pride with psychotic states when he notes:

> After searching for correlations between scores on the Sin Test and the diagnoses of psychiatric hospital patients, as well as correlations between Sin Test scores and MMPI scores, here is one of the findings: The psychiatric patients with the most prominent scores on the Pride Scale were those with more serious kinds of thinking disorders, including delusional beliefs, incompetent thinking, and poor reality testing. Those with schizophrenic and various brain syndrome diagnoses had significantly higher pride scores than other groups of psychiatric patients.[11]

Pride is self-focused. When we think incorrectly about other truths (such as 2 + 2 = 5), we might be participating in simple error or in a deliberate lie, but we aren't necessarily engaging in pride. But whenever our disordered thinking turns inward, pride surfaces. Sometimes we struggle to identify pride because it hides behind a façade of its opposite, humility.[12] A person who belittles himself and feels miserable in his discouragement may not be practicing humility but pride. If he's refusing God's assessment of his creatureliness, he is valuing his own opinion above God's. He's rejecting the truth of God's gracious disposition toward him. He's setting himself up as the final authority who has the right of self-determination, even to the point of suicide. His emotions might be despondent, but his mind is still raging against the limitations of his creatureliness. He truly hurts and feels "low," but his thoughts

---

[11] *What Your Counselor Never Told You*, 71.

[12] An excellent example of this phenomenon is Michael Eric Dyson, (*Pride: The Seven Deadly Sins* [Oxford: University Press, 2006]), who attacks the pride of some racial and social classes while exhibiting profound arrogance himself.

soar to such heights that he exalts his own right to do whatever he wants to do against all other claims, even God's. Whether we boast or shrivel up in discouragement, when we claim for ourselves any right or existence that we don't truly possess, we are proud.

A few more clarifications will sharpen our understanding of pride. Pride is slightly different from vainglory. Rebecca DeYoung distinguishes the two by observing that "pride excessively concerns excellence itself (excelling others); vainglory, by contrast, concerns primarily the display or manifestation of excellence . . . . Pride is a desire for genuine status; vainglory, a desire for recognition and acclaim."[13] Vainglory is more concerned about appearance than performance. In a separate book devoted to the topic of vainglory, DeYoung says, "The prideful desire superiority, and the vainglorious desire the show of superiority, although these can easily be entangled in practice."[14] These observations confirm our sense that pride is inaccurate thinking about oneself. Pride is actually believing that we're greater than, stronger than, and wiser than we really are. Vainglory is wanting other people to think that we're better than we really are. Pride says, "I am." Vainglory says, "Don't you think I am?"

> *A person who belittles himself may not be practicing humility but pride. If he's refusing God's assessment, he's valuing his own opinion above God's.*

KEY SCRIPTURE PASSAGES ON PRIDE

Although we sense the destructiveness and unwarrantedness of pride when we see it in others, we still cling to it as though

---

[13] Rebecca Konyndyk DeYoung, *Glittering Vices: A New Look at the Seven Deadly Sins and Their Remedies* (Grand Rapids: Brazos, 2009), 62.

[14] DeYoung, *Vainglory: The Forgotten Vice* (Grand Rapids: Eerdmans, 2014), 7–8.

we were an exception to the general rule. When Scripture confirms our suspicions and experience concerning the foolishness of pride, it destroys our excuses and leaves us with no further justification for this sin. In 1 Timothy 6:4 ("He is proud, knowing nothing"), the Bible confirms that pride stems from radically disoriented, incorrect thinking when it connects pride with a total lack of understanding. This is quite an assessment of the proud person. He thinks that he's wise, but God says he doesn't know anything. Pride blinds us to reality concerning ourselves and the world around us. Another passage warns that self-exaltation doesn't work because God won't allow us to puff ourselves up without His resisting our pride.

> All of you be subject one to another, and be clothed with humility: for God resisteth the proud, and giveth grace to the humble. Humble yourselves therefore under the mighty hand of God, that he may exalt you in due time. (1 Pet. 5:5–6)

Pride appears in numerous vice lists (Prov. 6:17–19; Mark 7:21–22; Rom. 1:28–32; 2 Tim. 3:2–7) and other negative contexts. The Bible never encourages it or merely channels it in more constructive directions. Pride has no place in the life of the believer.

When the men of Judah gathered to hear the Word of the Lord (Jer. 43:1–13), Jeremiah already had a record of prophesying accurately. He had correctly predicted the fall of Jerusalem to Nebuchadnezzar. He predicted the capture of Zedekiah, the slaughter of his sons, and the putting out of the king's eyes, all of which had happened. So when the rulers of the people asked Jeremiah what to do, and he urged them not to go into Egypt, we would expect them to obey. But they didn't listen. Their pride overrode reality and created an alternative world—a world in which their own imaginations controlled their circumstances.

> Then spake Azariah the son of Hoshaiah, and Johanan the son of Kareah, and all the proud men, saying unto Jeremiah, Thou speakest falsely: the Lord our God hath not sent thee to say, Go not into Egypt to sojourn there: but Baruch the son of Neriah setteth thee on against us, for to deliver us into the hand of the Chaldeans, that they might put us to death, and carry us away captives into Babylon. So Johanan the son of Kareah, and all the captains of the forces, and all the people, obeyed not the voice of the Lord, to dwell in the land of Judah. (Jer. 43:2–4)

They weren't in control of their circumstances, though. Their pride didn't change reality. Nebuchadnezzar brought his armies against Egypt and destroyed the people who thought they could safely disregard God's Word.

Pride originally arose in Satan's rebellion sometime after the creation, and its influence appears in many sins throughout Scripture. Satan appealed to Adam and Eve on the basis of not only their physical desires but also their pride. They followed the serpent in overreaching God's plan—warped in their thinking concerning their needs and rights. Pride united with anger in Moses' striking the rock as he, without any appeal to God's provision, said: "Hear now, ye rebels; must we fetch you water out of this rock?" (Num. 20:10). Pride stirred up Amaziah to attack an adversary much more powerful than he was, and so pride wrecked his wealth and power when he suffered defeat (2 Chron. 25:17–24). Virtually every sin and failure recorded in Scripture relates in some way to pride.

INTERCONNECTIONS WITH OTHER SINS

Pride rarely derives from other sins (though it certainly can be intensified by other sins). Instead, it seems to be the fountain of nearly all other sin. We should recognize the children of pride when we see them around us because its descendants are numerous. Pride is so self-assured of the correctness of its perceptions and the legitimacy of its rights that it is capable of every imaginable cruelty toward those who resist its claims. Pride drives tyrants to destroy millions of their citizens. Without pride, no dictator could value his own opinions so highly that his whims should supersede the lives of people. Pride drives reckless politicians to impose their petty prejudices on entire nations. (Of course, *they* see the issues clearly and know what's best for the rest of us.) Pride entrenches us so solidly in our opinions that we won't yield to reason or evidence to the contrary. "It produces high-blown, stiff-necked, puffed-up, and stuck-up people."[15] When wounded, pride reacts fiercely, stubbornly, and wrathfully.[16] Since it already thinks highly of itself without warrant to back that thinking, it permits no opposition. Adversaries must be ridden down and destroyed.[17]

The sins that most frequently attend pride appear in a key biblical illustration—the life of Nabal. As is true of much of the scriptural narrative, this passage doesn't directly state its theme, but the evidence for that theme is clear. Pride is folly, and the more stubbornly it is held, the greater the fool who holds it.

---

[15] Rick Ezell, *The Seven Sins of Highly Defective People* (Grand Rapids: Kregel, 2003), 16.

[16] Henry Fairlie, *The Seven Deadly Sins Today* (Washington, DC: New Republic Books, 1978), 89.

[17] W. H. Auden, "On Anger," in *The Seven Deadly Sins,* ed. Ian Fleming (New York: William Morrow and Company, 1962), 80.

Nabal exhibited the aggressive hostility that stems from thoroughly developed pride. God had blessed Nabal through both his physical location (good pastureland) and his heritage (he was a descendant of Caleb). David had protected Nabal from marauders and thieves. When David's men came to Nabal on a festival day (a traditional time for sharing in gratitude to God for all His gifts), Nabal didn't just send them away empty-handed, he insulted them severely. Samuel had already anointed David to be the next king of Israel. This fact was well enough known that Abigail, Nabal's wife, refers to it in her conversation with David (1 Sam. 25:30). David had also been fighting for God and the nation for several years (the victory over Goliath had occurred back in 1 Samuel 17). Hearing David's gracious request to share in God's blessings, Nabal attacked David as a nobody from nowhere. Asking "Who is David?" at a time when David's name was a household word in Israel was a petty, absurd insult; but Nabal went much further than this. He accused David of treason in claiming that David was breaking away from Saul by his own choice. Nabal added gross selfishness (notice that he included water among the things that he wouldn't share) and ingratitude toward God to his arrogance. He finished his tirade with deliberate unkindness, inhospitality, and indifference—leading even his own servants to comment on his worthlessness as a human being. In the entire diatribe, Nabal's egocentrism pours out like a flood. He illustrates the depths to which pride will sink in an attempt to exalt itself. (See Table 3.1.) The higher pride reaches, the meaner it appears to everyone else.

> *Pride is folly, and the more stubbornly it is held, the greater the fool who holds it.*

TABLE 3.1: SINS CONNECTED WITH PRIDE—THE LIFE OF NABAL

1 Samuel	Verse	Sin
25:10	Who is David? Who is the son of Jesse?	insulting
25:10	There be many servants now a days that break away every man from his master.	slander
25:11	Shall I then take my bread, and my water, and my flesh that I have killed for my shearers . . .	selfishness, ungratefulness
25:11	. . . and give it unto men . . .	unkindness, inhospitality
25:11	. . . whom I know not whence they be?	indifference
25:17	[The servants said] He is such a son of Belial, that a man cannot speak to him.	implacability

If pride distorts a person's thinking, he may view his own opinion and beliefs as infallible. In this case, whatever he desires becomes good to him. Pride justifies lust and gluttony on the grounds that since we are such exalted ones, we deserve to experience pleasure. Pride validates greed since we're worthy of possessing whatever would make us happy. Pride vindicates envy since we deserve greater applause, greater blessings, and greater opportunities than anyone else. After all, we're superior to everyone else. Pride rationalizes wrath since the failure of others to recognize our greatness amounts to stubborn wickedness on their part. And their stubbornness deserves our opposition. Pride can even excuse sloth since the despondent often believe that their misery derives from the failure of others to recognize how wonderful they are. Pride unbars the gate to all other sins. It's the great instigator and apologist for all sin.

The rest of Scripture demonstrates that pride leads directly to godlessness. And once a person has jettisoned God from his life, nothing stands in the way of any other evil. Table 3.2 depicts some of these connections. Pride is also prone to violence, at least verbal violence, and, if it has the power to get away with it, violence in actions as well. It violates the truth by representing the proud individual falsely, by slandering the good in others, and by abusing the standards of God. This is no trivial matter. Pride is one of the strongest strands in the web of iniquity that we spin in the dark corners of our lives.

TABLE 3.2: SINS CONNECTED WITH PRIDE—OTHER SCRIPTURES

References	Verse	Sin
Psalm 10:2	The wicked in his pride doth persecute the poor.	abuse
Psalm 10:4	The wicked, through the pride of his countenance, will not seek after God: God is not in all his thoughts.	godlessness
Psalm 86:14	O God, the proud are risen against me, and the assemblies of violent men have sought after my soul; and have not set thee before them.	violence godlessness
Psalm 119:51; 123:4	The proud have had me greatly in derision. Our soul is exceedingly filled with the scorning of those that are at ease, and with the contempt of the proud.	mockery, contempt
Psalm 119:69	The proud have forged a lie against me.	lying
Psalm 119:78	Let the proud be ashamed; for they dealt perversely with me without a cause.	injustice
Psalm 119:85; 140:5	The proud have digged pits for me. The proud have hid a snare for me, and cords; they have spread a net by the wayside; they have set gins for me.	injuring others by entrapment

References	Verse	Sin
Psalm 119:122	Let not the proud oppress me.	oppression
Proverbs 13:10; 28:25 1 Timothy 6:4	Only by pride cometh contention. He that is of a proud heart stirreth up strife. He is proud, knowing nothing, but doting about questions and strifes of words, whereof cometh envy, strife, railings, evil surmisings.	strife
Proverbs 21:24	Proud and haughty scorner is his name, who dealeth in proud wrath.	scorn, wrath
Isaiah 16:6 (cf. Jer. 48:29)	We have heard of the pride of Moab; he is very proud: even of his haughtiness, and his pride, and his wrath: but his lies shall not be so.	wrath, lying
Daniel 4:30	Is not this great Babylon, that I have built for the house of the kingdom by the might of my power, and for the honour of my majesty?	boasting
Obadiah 1:3	The pride of thine heart hath deceived thee.	deception
Zephaniah 2:10	This shall they have for their pride, because they have reproached and magnified themselves against the people of the Lord of hosts.	slander, boasting

Proverbs 13:10 provides an interesting insight. We already saw in Chapter 2 that envy frequently gives rise to strife and contention, but Solomon indicates that strife can arise only where pride exists. This means that pride accompanies envy whenever envy stirs up strife.[18] The two are inseparable.

---

[18] Backus observes that "verbal quarreling for some proud persons is very nearly their only conversational style" (62).

PRIDE TODAY

Like the cobwebs that form in every corner and every room in our houses no matter how often we clean them out, we continue to struggle with pride throughout our lives. Pride takes too many forms and camouflages itself in too many good causes for us to exterminate it completely and finally. We may participate in worthy social causes, such as serving in a soup kitchen or helping at an assisted living facility, and we may be doing so for all the right reasons. But pride is barely a step away. Though what we're doing is good, as soon as we consider ourselves spiritual because of our involvement in these causes, sin has sprung into our lives. Unrecognized and unattended, it attaches to other sins and becomes a serious snare.

We may serve the Lord through our schools and churches; but if at some point we begin to identify those institutions with the perfection of God's work on this earth, and if we start to identify ourselves too closely with these causes, our pride is pricked when

Pride is too strong a vice, too interconnected a web for us to let it go unrepented in our lives.

another church increases in size more rapidly than ours. And if anyone critiques the causes we're part of, we unleash a barrage of invective against him, at least secretly in our minds, as if he had attacked our very existence.

We're proud of our property, proud of our children, proud of our intelligence, and proud of our athletic, musical, or rhetorical skills. We take pride in our accomplishments, pride in our investments, pride in our allegiances, and pride in our popularity. When we bristle at critique, we exhibit pride. Either the critique is true, or it's false. If it's false, we can brush it off as irrelevant.

49

If it's true, we ought to take steps to correct what's wrong in our lives. But pride will not permit the suggestion that we are defective. We've spent our lives building up an image of our superiority, and our egos are bruised when anyone exposes that superiority to be a sham. If pride were to stand alone, it would still be a sin we need to repent of. But it doesn't stand alone. It calls wrath to its defense. It claims pleasure as its just due. It wields every weapon of violence that the arsenal of sin has ever seen. And it will not rest or be silent.

A grateful recognition of the gifts and opportunities that God has given is not pride. Humility doesn't lie. It doesn't pretend to lack what God has truly given. But humility recognizes the limitations of our knowledge, our strength, and our skill, whereas pride overreaches in all of these areas. We would think that as the desire to do righteousness grows in us, the tendency toward pride would decrease. But pride acts counterintuitively. As God actively sanctifies us, we draw closer to our proper humanity. We make real progress in the process of becoming what God intends for us to be. Yet as we draw nearer to this proper sphere, the tendency grows to compare ourselves to others who aren't yet as spiritually mature as we are. The web of pride ensnares us, and we soon get tangled up in other sins. Spiritual growth presents us with the opportunity of seeing ourselves soberly in light of the truth (Matt. 5:3) so that we neither diminish what we are in the eyes of God nor inflate ourselves beyond His assessment of us. While humility is keenly self-aware, pride remains ignorant of reality.

Paul warns spiritual leaders against the precipitous fall that occurs when they stray into pride. Since pride links immediately to every other sin, no level of maturity or length in ministry preserves us from catastrophic failure. "Wherefore let him that thinketh he standeth take heed lest he fall" (1 Cor. 10:12). Each of us must take this warning seriously. Pride is too strong a vice, too interconnected a web for us to let it go unrepented in our lives.

4

SLOTH—UNDERWHELMING APATHY

In the world it calls itself tolerance; but in hell it is called despair. It is the accomplice of the other sins and their worst punishment. It is the sin that believes in nothing, cares for nothing, seeks to know nothing, interferes with nothing, enjoys nothing, loves nothing, hates nothing, finds purpose in nothing, lives for nothing, and remains alive only because there is nothing it would die for.[1]

Sloth is probably the least understood of all the capital sins. Sure, those shiftless, lazy people who choose not to work are slothful, but not us. In assuming that only idle people are slothful, we've confused an effect (laziness) with its cause (sloth).[2] Our lack of understanding makes us wonder why theologians castigate a little indolence as severely as the sins of envy and lust. This seems unreasonable. Are we supposed to work our fingers to the bone every hour of the day and collapse from exhaustion? Do we have to feel guilty if we sit down to rest, to read a novel, or to play a game? If so, then any vacation, no matter how slight, plunges us into a capital vice. It's both relieving and intriguing to find out that sloth bears little resemblance to recreation.

---

[1] This frequently cited quotation about sloth comes from Dorothy Sayers, *The Whimsical Christian* (New York: Macmillan, 1978), 176. Sayers provides penetrating and witty analysis of this and the other six capital sins.

[2] "Sloth cannot be defined as laziness, since slothful people often pour great physical effort and emotional energy into the difficult task of distracting themselves from the unhappiness of their real condition." Rebecca Konyndyk DeYoung, *Glittering Vices: A New Look at the Seven Deadly Sins and Their Remedies* (Grand Rapids: Brazos, 2009), 89–90.

DEFINING SLOTH

Thomas Aquinas called sloth *tristitia de bono spirituali*—"sadness in the midst of spiritual good."[3] Aquinas's Roman Catholic theology contradicts important doctrines of Scripture, and he's by no means a model for Christians to follow. However, his treatment of certain specific sins provides valuable insight into their origin and consequences. As originally understood by the early church fathers, sloth had "two components: *acedia*, which means a lack of caring, an aimless indifference to one's responsibilities to God and to man, and *tristitia*, meaning sadness and sorrow leading to a final stage of despair."[4] Articulated in a single definition, sloth is dejection or apathy that finds no purpose or good in life as God has ordained it.[5]

> *It's both relieving and intriguing to find out that sloth bears little resemblance to recreation.*

Sloth can lead to inactivity (giving up in despair) or to restless hyperactivity (attempting to escape the boredom of life through busyness). Writers frequently use the following concepts in their definitions of sloth: alienation from God, lethargy, apathy, lukewarmness, lackadaisicalness, "grief, dejection, listlessness, restlessness, and psychic

---

[3] Aquinas's words are *tristitiam spirituali boni* and later as given above (*Summa Theologica*, Second Part, Question 35, Articles 1 & 2). The fact that Aquinas correctly identified the key components that comprise sloth and the fact that he articulated them cogently does not make his theology acceptable or commendable. He happens to have given us a particularly accurate description in this one realm of sin, but we do not endorse his person or theology.

[4] Rick Ezell, *The Seven Sins of Highly Defective People* (Grand Rapids: Kregel, 2003), 70.

[5] Fairlie provides a helpful supporting definition: "Sloth is a state of dejection that gives rise to torpor of mind and feeling and spirit; to a sluggishness or, as it has been put, a poisoning of the will; to despair; faintheartedness, and even desirelessness, a lack of real desire for anything, even for what is good." Henry Fairlie, *The Seven Deadly Sins Today* (Washington, DC: New Republic Books, 1978), 113.

exhaustion,"[6] distastefulness, repulsiveness, boredom, idleness, sadness, sorrow, weariness, despair, loathing, disgust, and bitterness at life.[7] When life seems unendurable, unbearable, burdensome, flavorless, or pointless, sloth has caught us in its web. We have given up on God's wisdom and grace and plunged into sustained despondency or aimlessness.

KEY SCRIPTURE PASSAGES ON SLOTH

While the Bible provides numerous examples of people who suffered from the sin of sloth, it tends to address the sins that stem from sloth more than the root sin, at least by overt terminology. A few key passages indicate a slackness of spirit and idleness of activity that are common to sloth. The people of Israel had escaped Egypt in the Exodus but then lapsed into sloth through their unbelief. God delivered them from slavery through great wonders and signs. He promised to give them Canaan, a land flowing with milk and honey. He had supported them and supplied their needs through manna and water from a rock. Yet the people balked when God commanded them to go up and take possession of the land. On the one hand were the clear evidences of God's presence, power, and provision; on the other hand were the uncertainties and difficulties that might attend the expulsion of the Canaanites. Instead of exercising faith in a God who had proven Himself repeatedly, the Israelites sank down into despondent spiritual stupor. They lifted up their voices and cried. The congregation was tired of manna, tired of the scrub plants in the desert, tired of the heat, tired of living in tents—in a word, tired of God's chosen method of provision.

---

[6] William Backus, *What Your Counselor Never Told You: Seven Secrets Revealed—Conquer the Power of Sin in Your Life* (Minneapolis: Bethany House, 2000), 147.

[7] See DeYoung, *Glittering Vices*, 83–84.

If sloth is dejection or apathy that finds no purpose or good in life as God has ordained it, we can't get a much clearer illustration of it than the words of the people: "All the children of Israel murmured against Moses and against Aaron: and the whole congregation said unto them, Would God that we had died in the land of Egypt! or would God we had died in this wilderness!" (Num. 14:2). The people were so slack-hearted that they actually preferred death to the life that God was promising them. Forty years later, Joshua warned the people against sloth when he urged, "How long are ye slack to go to possess the land, which the Lord God of your fathers hath given you?" (Josh. 18:3). The people of God never have the right to be filled with dejection and torpor since this kind of depression amounts to sloth, which is evidence of unbelief.

> *When life seems unendurable, unbearable, burdensome, flavorless, or pointless, sloth has caught us in its web.*

Nine hundred years later, in 539 BC, God fulfilled His promises to Jeremiah and the people of Israel by bringing them back from the Babylonian captivity (Jer. 29:10). God promised the blessing of His presence and favor, and He had proven His Word to be true when the people returned from Babylon. But the people still faced the temptation of sloth. When they returned to Jerusalem, the city and the temple lay in ruins. Rebuilding was hard. Opposition arose from the surrounding pagan nations: "Then the people of the land weakened the hands of the people of Judah, and troubled them in building" (Ezra 4:4). Later, when rebuilding the wall, the people said, "For they all made us afraid, saying, Their hands shall be weakened from the work, that it be not done" (Neh. 6:9). The "weakness" that ensued was sloth. The task was too hard and the opposition too great—"there's no point in trying to rebuild because we can't succeed against such adversity." Ezra and Nehemiah strove against such dejection and apathy by countering the people's misguided thinking with the great truth that God is with us.

In the New Testament parable of the talents (Matt. 25:14–30), the servant who buried his talent in the earth did so out of imagined fears. He shirked his proper responsibility and settled into dejected idleness: "There's no point in trying because I'll probably fail anyway, and then my master will take it out on me. It's better just to bury the talent and sit here." We might think that the servant was simply lazy except for his own words that reveal his thinking:

> Lord, I knew thee that thou art an hard man, reaping where thou hast not sown, and gathering where thou hast not strawed: and I was afraid, and went and hid thy talent in the earth. (Matt. 25:24–25)

The servant had experienced good. He had his master's trust; he had opportunity; he had time; and he had a reasonable master who wisely gave in direct proportion to each servant's ability. But this slothful servant threw it all away. Instead of being thrilled with the blessing, he sank down in dejection and apathy—paralyzed by the circumstances of life that God had ordained for him.

Most Christians don't realize that one of the severest warning passages in the book of Hebrews points toward sloth as the cause of apostasy:

> It is impossible for those who were once enlightened, and have tasted of the heavenly gift, and were made partakers of the Holy Ghost, and have tasted the good word of God, and the powers of the world to come, if they shall fall

away, to renew them again unto repentance; seeing they crucify to themselves the Son of God afresh, and put him to an open shame. For the earth which drinketh in the rain that cometh oft upon it, and bringeth forth herbs meet for them by whom it is dressed, receiveth blessing from God: but that which beareth thorns and briers is rejected, and is nigh unto cursing; whose end is to be burned. But, beloved, we are persuaded better things of you, and things that accompany salvation, though we thus speak. For God is not unrighteous to forget your work and labour of love, which ye have shewed toward his name, in that ye have ministered to the saints, and do minister. And we desire that every one of you do shew the same diligence to the full assurance of hope unto the end: that ye be not slothful, but followers of them who through faith and patience inherit the promises. (Heb. 6:4–12)

Why would anyone fall away from the promises of God concerning salvation? If a person comes to believe that there is no hope for him to experience those promises (6:4–6), if he produces no good that corresponds to the blessings he has received (6:7–8), and if he gives up on the spiritual life because he thinks God is too harsh to merit his trust (6:10), sloth has eaten away his defective faith and exposed it as the unbelief that it really is. Sloth proves to be a deadly, damning sin. We cannot afford to treat it as anything less than the terrible vice that it is.

INTERCONNECTIONS WITH OTHER SINS

King David lived a life of action. He fought the Philistines, the Edomites, the Moabites, the Ammonites, and the Amalekites. He led military special ops. He executed tactical maneuvers, succeeded against all odds, and unified the people. He was likeable, passionate, gregarious, and magnetic. But when he sank into sloth at one stage of life, it plunged his family into ruin and blighted his legacy. Ask any well-informed student of Scripture what David's great sin was, and you'll get a decisive answer—adultery with Bathsheba. But that adultery didn't just "spring out of nowhere." It resulted from sloth. Enough evidence exists in 2 Samuel 11 to demonstrate that David neglected his duty during a bout of spiritual torpor.

To begin with, 11:1 provides the brief comment that these events occurred "at the time when kings go forth to battle." Instead of fulfilling his God-ordained role, David sent Joab in his place. This wasn't a single battle. It was a full-scale military campaign that followed the Ammonites' brutal dishonor of David's servants in 2 Samuel 10. David didn't miss just a day or a week at the head of his army. He missed months. God had made David a man of war and of action, but now the king was languishing in Jerusalem. God had also appointed David to fight against pagan adversaries who dishonored God and His people, but David was apparently tired of this responsibility and handed it over to a subordinate.

Next, 2 Samuel 11:2 tells us, "In an eveningtide, . . . David arose from off his bed." David wasn't ill. He shouldn't have been lounging around all day long only to get out of bed in the late afternoon. Finally, Scripture indicates that David was bored. He was walking around looking for something, for anything to do. Later, Nathan's rebuke of David completes the argument. He drew the king's attention to the blessings that God had given him (12:7–8). Nathan also leveled the accusation from God, "Thou hast despised me" (12:10). Tying all of these biblical evidences together we might well ask what sin is apathetic toward duty, lazes around the house, looks for anything amusing to distract it, and slights the blessings of God. The answer is sloth.

Sloth proves itself to be a strong and ensnaring web. The sins that attend sloth in the life of David count among the most serious offenses known to man. (See Table 4.1.) Numerous sins of David's descendants and friends resulted from David's sloth. While it isn't our purpose to explore at length the sins in other people's lives that are caused by our sins, we can observe that the influence of David's sloth runs from 2 Samuel 11 to 2 Samuel 19 and includes Amnon's rape of Tamar, Absalom's murder of Amnon, David's refusal to execute justice against either son, Absalom's conspiracy, the revolt of the nation, the lies of Ziba, the financial injury to Mephibosheth, the suicide of Ahithophel, and the murder of Absalom. Had David remained actively committed to God's work instead of apathetic toward it, he might have staved off this onslaught of ruin. Sloth is no small sin. We who are God's children cannot pass over it in ignorance or indifference. Sloth has the power to corrupt our thinking so badly that any sin is possible to us.

TABLE 4.1: SINS CONNECTED WITH SLOTH—THE LIFE OF DAVID

2 Samuel	Verse	Sin
11:4 (cf. 12:9)	He lay with her.	adultery
11:6	David sent to Joab, saying, Send me Uriah the Hittite.	conspiracy
11:13	He made him drunk.	inducing drunkenness
11:14	David wrote a letter to Joab, and sent it by the hand of Uriah.	callousness

2 Samuel	Verse	Sin
11:15 (cf. 12:9)	Set ye Uriah in the forefront of the hottest battle, and retire ye from him, that he may be smitten, and die.	murder
11:27	But the thing that David had done displeased the Lord.	godlessness
12:4	[He] took the poor man's lamb.	theft
12:5	As the Lord liveth, the man that hath done this thing shall surely die.	injustice in judgment
12:14	Thou hast given great occasion to the enemies of the Lord to blaspheme.	inciting blasphemy

Like David, Elijah was a man of action. He fearlessly approached Ahab to declare the word of the Lord (1 Kings 17:1). He confronted the king, the prophets and priests of Baal, and all the people at Carmel (1 Kings 18:17–39). He killed the prophets of Baal (1 Kings 18:40). He anointed prophets and kings (1 Kings 19:15–17). He declared the Lord's curse on Ahab for his murder of Naboth (1 Kings 21:20–22). And he prophesied the death of Ahaziah (2 Kings 1:3–4). This was a man who couldn't be stopped by external adversaries. He wasn't afraid of kings; he wasn't ultimately fixated on polls and popularity; and he was passionately devoted to God and God's work. Elijah seems an unlikely candidate for a sin such as sloth, but right in the middle of these passages about his ministry, Scripture records that Elijah succumbed to despondent inactivity in spite of God's good work. Instead of remembering the power and goodness of God, Elijah could see only the bleakness of national sin and failure. Table 4.2 presents the series of sins that accompanied Elijah's sloth.

TABLE 4.2: SINS CONNECTED WITH SLOTH—THE LIFE OF ELIJAH

1 Kings	Verse	Sin
19:3	He arose, and went for his life.	fear of man
19:4	He requested for himself that he might die.	death wish from despair
19:4	I am not better than my fathers.	pride
19:10, 14	And I, even I only, am left.	misrepresenting truth

Both David and Elijah demonstrate that sloth does not have to be an entrenched disposition or an entire life's pattern in order to wreak havoc on our spiritual health. Both of these men succumbed to sloth after years of diligence, faithfulness, and obedience. Evidently, while a slothful disposition might be more prone to apathy and disgust with life, even those who participate actively in God's plan can fall quickly. This makes sloth a particular threat to faithful believers. We can resist Satan's attacks and advance the kingdom of God through the power and indwelling of the Holy Spirit for many years. But if at some point we yield to the self-pitying discouragement that contradicts God's blessing on our lives, a fall from great heights of godliness and usefulness can occur in a moment. Numerous other passages of Scripture complete the picture of the web that springs from sloth. (See Table 4.3 on the next page).

TABLE 4.3: SINS CONNECTED WITH SLOTH—OTHER SCRIPTURES

References	Verse	Sin
Proverbs 18:9	He also that is slothful in his work is brother to him that is a great waster.	destruction of good
Proverbs 24:30–31	I went by the field of the slothful, and by the vineyard of the man void of understanding; And, lo, it was all grown over with thorns, and nettles had covered the face thereof, and the stone wall thereof was broken down.	
Ecclesiastes 10:18	By much slothfulness the building decayeth; and through idleness of the hands the house droppeth through.	
Proverbs 21:25–26	The desire of the slothful killeth him; for his hands refuse to labour. He coveteth greedily all the day long.	covetousness
Proverbs 26:16	The sluggard is wiser in his own conceit than seven men that can render a reason.	self-deception, pride

SLOTH TODAY

Sloth is a chronic sin of the industrialized, high-tech world. Humanity typically does not use its leisure time well. Instead of reflecting on and rejoicing in the good that God has done, we tend to pursue idle or active entertainment. After we've caught up on the latest thrillers, gone to the mall a few times, and checked our social media status for the twelfth time today, we sit around listless and restless. Children rejoice when school gets out for the summer, but within a week every parent hears the plaintive, drawn-out complaint, "I'm bored. There's nothing to do." With rooms full of books and toys and with friends just minutes away down the street, they still can't find anything that piques their interest. And it's not just the children. Adults discuss vacation plans only to say, "No, let's not go there; we've been there *twice* already"—exaggerating the number of repeated visits to emphasize the absolute boredom that we would face if we had to go *there* again. People are bored in their jobs, bored with their houses, bored with their cars, and bored with their entertainment. We demand more to fill our idle minds—though idleness is more a symptom than the underlying cause of our ennui, our settled state of dejection and boredom. We move faster, live grander, and die sadder than many previous generations. In spite of all of our busyness, we never meet our full spiritual potential. We exhibit world-weariness, but then we look to the world to relieve our malaise. When the world offers no solutions that work, our dejection grows. "What's the use?" "What's the point in trying?" "There's nothing that matters." All of this is sloth.

Sloth stems from other sins and leads to other sins. Greed produces sloth in the end since the acquisition of far more than we really need for life tends to blunt the vibrancy of life itself. Recently my son and I played a video game that involved collecting coins in order to buy other characters. As I darted around getting as much play money as I could, he complained, "Let's not get so much money." "Why?" I asked. "Because once we have too much money, we can buy all the characters and all the extra abilities, and then the game is no fun anymore," he replied. No fun? Having too much results in aimlessness. Dejection to the point of boredom can stem from the greedy acquisition of material things. Envy also leads to sloth because it so poisons our outlook on life that we live for nothing other than to nurse our malice. We no longer see the

> *The people of God never have the right to be filled with dejection and torpor since this kind of depression amounts to sloth, which is evidence of unbelief.*

good that God has made; we see only the evil. Lust produces sloth, in the end, because we blunt the physical-emotional pleasure that God intends for an exclusive marital relationship. Overindulgence, including any type of gratification that is contrary to God's Word, results in a jaded attitude toward any good thing.

Sloth destroys many marriages. First love cools. Routines wear away the initial thrill of a new life together. Little irritations sap our zeal. Instead of viewing regularity as a sign of stability, strength, and faithfulness, we begin to see it as boring, uninteresting, and unsatisfying. What God has given to us as a blessing, we use to justify our listlessness and apathy. Instead of looking for a younger, leaner, prettier, smarter, more handsome, or more gregarious person, we have the privilege of rejoicing in the blessings that God has given us in a spouse that we have grown to know.

Sloth erodes ministry by viewing its repetitiveness as boring and mind numbing. It impels the pastor to abandon one ministry for greener pastures every five to ten years. It bores the teacher with a lesson that she is repeating for the fifteenth time. Everything we used to celebrate becomes tedious. Sighing, we cast our eyes downward in gloomy languor—seeing only the mundaneness of life and not its beauty. Sloth is a great adversary to all faithfulness. It grumbles at goodness. It lies about God by calling His loving-kindness into question.

Often slackness creeps into the duties of life because of emotional or physical threats to our well-being that make us want to quit. We think, "What use is it to do right when with the stroke of a pen a single wicked ruler can more than undo all the virtue that we have sought for our country?" "What is the point of working so hard when the manipulative, flattering, obsequious, flashy coworker always gets the promotions?" "Why pray, when God almost always answers no?" These causes of discouragement come from outside of ourselves. Pretending that these pains do not exist will not help. Pain and frustration are real, and we often have a very good reason to sense that something is out of joint. But the disgust with life that festers in our hearts when we focus on the shameful, the hurtful, the ruinous, and the vain things around us morphs into paralyzing sloth. Slowly our hearts turn away from confidence in God to apathy toward Him, and apathy is only a short step from rejecting Him altogether.

Sloth eats away at the life of the Christian teen, college student, or newly minted graduate who fails to recognize the good hand of God in his upbringing and training. He finds the Christian life as lived by his parents and pastor to be tedious and boring—too much talk of faithfulness, too little excitement; too many rules, too little freedom; too much predictability, too little spontaneity. He doesn't recognize in himself the symptoms of sloth, and so he turns away from genuine godliness in favor of a worldly religious excitement that can be found in any number of popular churches that cater to the whims and wishes of their attendees. Sure, he can justify his choices on the basis of the sins and inconsistencies in spiritual leaders of his

> *If a person . . . gives up on the spiritual life because he thinks God is too harsh to merit his trust, sloth has eaten away his defective faith and exposed it as the unbelief that it really is.*

past, but his apathy toward holiness as defined by God and toward the duties of the Christian life may well be thinly veiled sloth. It *is* easier to capitulate to the world than to persevere in God's commands. Life *doesn't* always present us with a thrill-a-minute path of spiritual growth. We *do* meet serious obstacles and discouragements.

But none of these ought to create in us a state of dejection in the face of the spiritual good that God has given us. Instead of regretting the spiritual upbringing we have received and despising the leaders God has set over us, we ought to recognize the grace of God. Confronting sloth in our hearts would curtail much of our rebellion.

Sloth is only a thought away. Like a weed, it needs no cultivation in order to take root. Like a web, it wraps itself around our lives, entangles our thoughts, and drags us toward spiritual death. In the book of Ecclesiastes, Solomon's expressions of frustration with life point us toward the solution. He tried to find meaning in work, sex, food, and every other "good" known to man, but he found all of these things to be tedious and vain. He discovered purpose and value in accepting and rejoicing in the good that God had given.

> Every man also to whom God hath given riches and wealth, and hath given him power to eat thereof, and to take his portion, and to rejoice in his labour; this is the gift of God. For he shall not much remember the days of his life; because God answereth him in the joy of his heart. (Eccles. 5:19–20)

Instead of grasping for more, delight in what you have. Instead of finding life tedious, consider its joys. Instead of responding to troubles with dejection, trust the Lord for the measure that He has apportioned to you. We lift up our faces, brighten our eyes, and invigorate our minds by consciously reveling in the good that God has given us, especially in Christ. If we leave the strands of sloth in our hearts, we will find them growing into a sprawling web of iniquity that draws us into numerous other sins.

5

GREED— AN ENTITLEMENT MINDSET

> Avarice is, not so much the love of possessions, as the love merely of possessing. To buy what we do not need, more even than we need for our pleasure or entertainment, is a love of possessing for its own sake.[1]

Fallen people can warp love so badly that they no longer direct it toward God and others at all. Affections that could create warm personal relationships latch onto material possessions instead, and greed is born. Avarice peers at the world through cold, glittering eyes. It sees people as a means to the end of acquiring its true love—money.

DEFINING GREED

Greed is the insatiable desire to acquire more than we currently possess. It invests supreme value in material things to such an extent that the acquisition of things becomes the solution to every problem and the central love of the heart. Fundamentally, greed is idolatry (Col. 3:5). It strokes its stacked coins and runs its eyes over the objects in its house to savor the feelings of luxury, security, and superiority that the possession of these things bring. It aligns closely with covetousness, which is the desire to acquire a particular thing that someone else already possesses. Greed is the underlying appetite. Covetousness is a thirst for what someone else has. We reproach greed in others, but we all want the opportunity

---

[1] Henry Fairlie, *The Seven Deadly Sins Today* (Washington, DC: New Republic Books, 1978), 135.

to try it for ourselves. Other people have been ruined by winning the lottery or striking it rich, but not us. We would invest wisely (of course, we would have to diversify, assure our future financial security for the rest of life, and quit work), buy only what we really need (a new car, new yacht and motorhome, a vacation home at the beach and another in the mountains, and a new wardrobe since ours is completely worn out), and give most of the money away (at least to the deserving, of which, come to think of it, we cannot recall any good examples).

The insatiability of greed is legendary. At this writing, four of the world's wealthiest financiers each has a net worth of at least $50 billion. That's 50,000 million dollars. If a person lives seventy years, his life spans only 25,550 days. These ultra-wealthy individuals would have had to spend $2 million per day every

> *We reproach greed in others, but we all want the opportunity to try it for ourselves.*

day since they were born until the day they die in order to spend that much money. Yet we see little evidence that they're content with what they've acquired. Several of them are on record talking about having enough, but they return to the markets to grasp for more—frequently destroying competing companies and stamping out jobs in the process. Greed is never satisfied with its acquisitions; so it must pursue more.

KEY SCRIPTURE PASSAGES ON GREED

Probably the most familiar verse in the Bible that touches on greed is 1 Timothy 6:10, "For the love of money is the root of all evil: which while some coveted after, they have erred from the faith, and pierced themselves through with many sorrows." Notice the immediate attention that the verse gives to the human disposition toward the use of money. Gold is amoral; silver has no virtue or vice. But our attitudes toward these resources have ethical implications. In fact, as moral beings, we always treat money (and all possessions for that matter) either righteously or sinfully. In every circumstance, we have either a right or wrong disposition toward money and other property. We either use it as God intended or as He did not intend. First Timothy 6:10 also confirms the theme of this book—that sin is actually a web of interconnected sins. Loving money, one form of being greedy, gives rise to all kinds of other sins.

The Bible teaches us that greed dehumanizes us because it reduces our value to the things that we possess. Jesus said, "Take heed, and beware of covetousness: for a man's life consisteth not in the abundance of the things which he possesseth" (Luke 12:15). We instinctively but sinfully value people based on their possessions. Those with more wealth command our respect, attention, and friendship (hence the stern warnings in James 2:1–9 against partiality toward the wealthy). They also command our allegiance and sometimes obedience. The poor command neither. Through greed we have equated our humanity with our assets. This defaces and defames the image of God in man, and thereby slanders the Creator. Greed drives people to acquire things at any cost to humanity. Proverbs 1:18–19 warns about the rich, "They lay wait for their own blood; they lurk privily for their own lives. So are the ways of every one that is greedy of gain; which taketh away the life of the owners thereof." Even if acquisitiveness does not result in overt physical self-harm, it always "murders" civility and humanity.

In God's estimation, greed disqualifies a person from public office (Exod. 18:21). God thought greed serious enough to devote the tenth commandment to its offshoot sin of covetousness (Exod. 20:17; Deut. 5:21). Two arguments lead us to conclude that

God's prohibition of covetousness is also a prohibition of greed. First, since a person cannot be covetous without also exhibiting an underlying disposition of greed, the causal sin (greed) is at least as serious a threat. Second, when Jesus intensified the law in Matthew 5, He indicated that the evil dispositions behind our sins make us just as guilty before God as the outward acts of sin. The law can judge and punish only outward acts, but inward dispositions defile us just as much. Wherever God prohibits covetousness, He's also prohibiting greed.

> *Through greed we have equated our humanity with our assets. This defaces and defames the image of God in man, and thereby slanders the Creator.*

When greed infects religious leaders, they tend to become hirelings—telling the people whatever the people want to hear so that the leaders can make a profit. Avarice was among the sins for which God sent Judah into captivity.

> Therefore will I give their wives unto others, and their fields to them that shall inherit them: for every one from the least even unto the greatest is given to covetousness, from the prophet even unto the priest every one dealeth falsely. (Jer. 8:10)

Numerous examples of greed appear in Scripture with little direct comment on the vice itself. Joshua 7 records how one man's greed led to the death of thirty-six other men (7:5), the destruction of all his possessions (7:15), and the loss of his own life and the lives of his children (7:25). Greed spawned theft (stealing from that which was devoted to God) and lying by covering up sin. Achan knew that his avarice was sin; otherwise he wouldn't have hidden the treasures in his tent. But he didn't properly gauge the seriousness of greed in God's eyes. From his perspective, it couldn't hurt to take a little reward for his part in the battle against Jericho. It didn't do anyone any good to burn up the treasures or bury them under a pile of rubble, and it wouldn't do any harm to take them for himself. But injury came swiftly on the heels of his greed. Achan didn't foresee the consequences that would follow his sin. All he could see was the benefit. We must never harbor the thought that the benefits of sin might outweigh its devastating consequences.

Ahab's greed drove his acquisition of Naboth's property (1 Kings 21). The passage shows Ahab's utter indifference to people. He didn't care how he acquired the property as long as he took possession of it. He seems to have maintained a studied ignorance of Jezebel's plot in an attempt to distance himself from the means of acquisition—the murder of Naboth. In his opinion, as long as he was able to feast on the delicacy he sought, the lives, rights, and inheritance of other people were merely a casualty of doing business. God was not fooled. As 1 Kings 21:19 demonstrates, God holds those who are greedy accountable for the consequences of their greed. Ahab might not have murdered Naboth directly, but God still found him guilty:

> Thus saith the Lord, Hast thou killed, and also taken possession? And thou shalt speak unto him, saying, Thus saith the Lord, In the place where dogs licked the blood of Naboth shall dogs lick thy blood, even thine. (1 Kings 21:19)

Scripture encourages us with the thought that "godliness with contentment is great gain" (1 Tim. 6:6) and never condones an insatiable appetite for more. While it points us toward a settled disposition ("Having food and raiment let us be therewith content"; 1 Tim. 6:8), it never encourages the inner turmoil that results from our inability to keep up with our neighbors in the acquisition of more stuff. Ultimately, avarice destroys: "They that will be rich fall into temptation and a snare, and into many foolish and hurtful lusts, which drown men in destruction and perdition" (1 Tim. 6:9), and God does not seek the ruin of His servants.

INTERCONNECTIONS WITH OTHER SINS

Like the other six capital sins, greed cannot abide solitude. It keeps company with the worst of sins:

> For the wicked boasts of the desires of his soul, and the one greedy for gain curses and renounces the Lord. (Ps. 10:3, ESV)

> We shall find all precious substance, we shall fill our houses with spoil . . . . Their feet run to evil, and make haste to shed blood. . . . So are the ways of every one that is greedy of gain; which taketh away the life of the owners thereof. (Prov. 1:13, 16, 19)

Greed also interweaves itself directly with other sins as either their cause or their effect. John Cassian observes, "For [greed] is a regular nest of sins, and a 'root of all kinds of evil,' and becomes a hopeless incitement to wickedness."[2] Cassian's analysis of greed's

---

[2] John Cassian, *The Works of John Cassian*, vol. 11 of *A Select Library of the Nicene and Post-Nicene Fathers of the Christian Church*, trans. Edgar C. S. Gibson, ed. Philip Schaff and Henry Wace (Buffalo, NY: Christian Literature Publishing Company, 1894), VII.6, http://biblehub.com/library/cassian/the_works_of_john_cassian_/chapter_vii_of_the_source.htm. While Cassian was a monastic whose renunciation of all material goods doesn't accord well with numerous passages of Scripture concerning the blessings of God, his analysis is still sound. He personally chose to renounce the goods of the

connections with other sins is insightful. Table 5.1 condenses and categorizes the sins that he observed relating to greed.[3]

Table 5.1: Sins Connected with Greed
(as analyzed by John Cassian)

Location	Citation	Sin
VII.1	"originating only from the state of a corrupt and sluggish mind"	sloth as the cause of greed
VII.7	"This vice has got hold of the slack and lukewarm soul."	
VII.7	"giving him excellent and almost reasonable excuses"	rationalization
VII.7	"What is provided . . . is not sufficient."	discontentment
VII.8	"like a bad-tempered horse, dashes off headlong and unbridled: and discontented with his daily food and usual clothing"	
VII.7	"What is he to do if ill health comes on, and he has no special store of his own to support him in his weakness?"	fear, anxiety
	"The wretched soul is agitated, and held fast, as it were, in a serpent's coils, while it endeavours to add to that heap which it has unlawfully secured, by still more unlawful care."	
VII.7	"a wretched and wearisome existence without making the slightest advance"	pride of life
VII.7	"He cannot without indignity be supported by another's substance, as a pauper and one in want."	pride
	"He has no scruples about transgressing the bounds of humility."	

world because of the claim that they had on him earlier in life, and he recognized the threat that greed is to the people of God. We don't have to advocate or follow his attitude toward the total rejection of material goods in order to recognize the threat of material greed.

[3] Ibid., VII.7–10.

Location	Citation	Sin
VII.7	"selling it secretly, and so securing the coveted coin"	hypocrisy, lying
VII.9	"Though he has a supply of money secretly hidden, yet he complains that he has neither shoes nor clothes."	
VII.7	"being entirely absorbed in the quest of gain, pays attention to nothing but how to get money"	idolatry
	"Through it all gold and the love of gain become to him his god."	
	"By the voice of the Apostle it is actually declared to be the worship of idols and false gods."	
VII.7	"never keeping faith where there is a gleam of hope of money to be got"	truce-breaking
VII.7	"For this it shrinks not from the crime of lying, perjury, and theft, of breaking a promise, of giving way to injurious bursts of passion."	lying, perjury, theft, anger
VII.8	"at last cares not to retain I will not say the virtue but even the shadow of humility, charity, and obedience"	indifference toward good
VII.8	"is displeased with everything, and murmurs and groans over every work"	complaining
VII.8	"having cast off all reverence"	irreverent
VII.9	"He answers impertinently."	insolence
VII.9	"Whatever he sees needing improvement, he despises and treats with contempt."	contempt
VII.9	"If . . . some of these are given first to one who is known to have nothing whatever, he is still more inflamed with burning rage."	selfish, self-serving anger
	"Of set purpose he looks out for opportunities of being offended and angry."	

Location	Citation	Sin
VII.9	"Nor is he contented to turn his hand to any work."	laziness
VII.9	"He never stops corrupting as many as he can by clandestine conferences." "never stops sowing and exciting discontent"	seduction, corruption of others
VII.10	"It suffers him to keep no services of prayer, no system of fasting, no rule of vigils; it does not allow him to fulfil the duties of seemly intercession, if only he can satisfy the madness of avarice."	loss of worship and devotion

Although greed is a major strand in the web of sin, it frequently has its origin in other sins. Proverbs 21:25–26 seems to indicate that sloth can either give rise to greed or attend it closely: "The desire of the slothful killeth him; for his hands refuse to labour. He coveteth greedily all the day long." Common human experience has observed that selfishness and pride give rise to greed. If we focus reflexively on ourselves and demand a good life for ourselves, the next natural question is "What contributes to the good life?" Since money does such a good job of purchasing and providing security, ease, comfort, friends, food, and possessions, it seems to be the most natural direction for the selfish heart to go.[4] In fact, it's nearly impossible to envision a humble person being greedy. Our greed may coldly trample the rights of others in order to secure our rights. It may acquire the property of others in order to expand our own properties. And it may encroach on the stability and security of others in order to guarantee our security.

---

[4] Rebecca Konyndyk DeYoung observes, "Greed is the root of all kinds of evil, because it is itself rooted in pride." *Glittering Vices: A New Look at the Seven Deadly Sins and Their Remedies* (Grand Rapids: Brazos, 2009), 111.

Several key biblical examples confirm the link between greed and other sins. Sometimes this connection is so direct that the resultant sins seem highly blameworthy to the onlooker. But the life of Lot demonstrates that greed can give rise to other sins even when the greedy person didn't intend for the other sins to occur. That Lot was greedy is hard to dispute. When Abraham sought to resolve the conflict between his own herdsmen and those of Lot, he gave Lot the privilege of first choice of land.

> Lot lifted up his eyes, and beheld all the plain of Jordan, that it was well watered every where, before the Lord destroyed Sodom and Gomorrah, even as the garden of the Lord, like the land of Egypt, as thou comest unto Zoar. Then Lot chose him all the plain of Jordan; and Lot journeyed east: and they separated themselves the one from the other. (Gen. 13:10–11)

Of course, Lot chose shrewdly. Could we really expect otherwise? Was he supposed to take the worst land? Lot was the younger relative. Civility in the ancient Near East required him to take second place, but greed leaps at the opportunity for gain regardless of any offense to politeness or courtesy. In a roughly analogous situation in Genesis 23, Abraham asked to buy Ephron's cave in order to bury Sarah. Ephron responded in a fashion that is surprising to us. He urged Abraham to take the field and cave rather than to buy them (23:11). This was an offer of civility and hospitality that showed respect to the dead (Sarah) and to the one who was grieving (Abraham). Unlike Lot, Abraham recognized the gracious gesture for what it was, and he insisted on paying full price for the land (23:16) rather than taking advantage of Ephron's generosity. Imagine Lot's having the same opportunity! He would have jumped at the chance to get land for free just as he did years earlier when offered such a choice by Abraham. As Table 5.2 depicts, many sins followed on the heels of Lot's greed.

TABLE 5.2: SINS CONNECTED WITH GREED—THE LIFE OF LOT

Genesis	Verse	Sin
13:12	Lot dwelled in the cities of the plain, and pitched his tent toward Sodom.	compromise
19:8	Behold now, I have two daughters which have not known man; let me, I pray you, bring them out unto you, and do ye to them as is good in your eyes.	betrayal, cruelty, pragmatism
19:8	Only unto these men do nothing; for therefore came they under the shadow of my roof.	reversal of values
19:14	But he seemed as one that mocked unto his sons in law.	loss of moral standing
19:19	I cannot escape to the mountain, lest some evil take me, and I die.	fear, love of security
19:31–32	The firstborn said unto the younger, Our father is old, and there is not a man in the earth to come in unto us after the manner of all the earth: come, let us make our father drink wine, and we will lie with him, that we may preserve seed of our father.	corruption of the following generation
19:33, 35	They made their father drink wine that night, and the firstborn went in, and lay with her father. . . and the younger arose, and lay with him.	drunkenness, immorality

The Bible also shows us that greed effected the darkest moment in human history. Without Judas Iscariot's greed, a long chain of events would have had to have happened differently. Greed drove Judas to the most unconscionable of sins and finally to his death at his own hands. His behavior leading up to the pivotal moment of betrayal gave no indication of the audacity of greed. No one besides Jesus suspected Judas of being capable of such cross materialism that he would sell the Lord for the price of a slave. Table 5.3 depicts the catastrophic consequences that greed had in the life of Judas, and it warns us against the presumption that we can escape the spirals of sins that connect with greed.

TABLE 5.3: SINS CONNECTED WITH GREED—THE LIFE OF JUDAS

Matthew	Verse	Sin
26:9 (cf. John 12:5–6)	This ointment might have been sold for much, and given to the poor. (This [Judas] said, not that he cared for the poor; but because he was a thief, and had the bag, and bare what was put therein.)	theft
26:15	What will ye give me, and I will deliver him unto you? And they covenanted with him for thirty pieces of silver.	betrayal
26:16	From that time he sought opportunity to betray him.	manipulative treachery
26:25	Then Judas, which betrayed him, answered and said, Master, is it I?	hypocrisy, deceit
26:48–49	Whomsoever I shall kiss, that same is he: hold him fast. And forthwith he came to Jesus, and said, Hail, master; and kissed him.	jaded cynicism, deceit, hypocrisy
27:1	When the morning was come, all the chief priests and elders of the people took counsel against Jesus to put him to death.	complicity in injustice, murder
27:5	He cast down the pieces of silver in the temple, and departed, and went and hanged himself.	despair, suicide

Centuries of human behavior have compiled a case against greed. We can indict it for its direct connection with virtually every other sin. Note the litany of abuses ascribed to greed: "Having more money than you need can lead to arrogance, showing off, free rein to lust, unbridled pursuit of entertainment, frequent or constant desire for illicit pleasure, and proud condescension toward people who have less."[5] The vices that spring from greed, says another writer, "include theft and fraud and robbery—all of which are means to acquire more wealth or stuff. Greed also spawns restlessness and callousness toward those in need, vices which are the effects of greed's perpetual escalation of desire and discontentment and its focus on material things as objects that can be controlled and secured for one's own possession."[6] A well-known preacher warns: "Avarice seeks more than its own in life. It cheats, robs, murders and slanders to achieve its desires."[7] One social critic said that greed, similar to the other six vices, "is likely to cause us to be cruel"[8] and "may easily lead to [wrath], if it is balked."[9]

Scripture proves that what human experience has revealed about greed is accurate. Table 5.4 demonstrates the pervasive evil that accompanies greed. We may not all exhibit every trait, but the web of sin is so extensive and pervasive that we cannot tolerate greed in our lives without falling into its numerous traps.

---

[5] William Backus, *What Your Counselor Never Told You: Seven Secrets Revealed—Conquer the Power of Sin in Your Life* (Minneapolis: Bethany House, 2000), 128.

[6] Rebecca Konyndyk DeYoung, *Vainglory: The Forgotten Vice* (Grand Rapids: Eerdmans, 2014), 56–57. Great literary works agree. See Emma B. Hawkins, "Tolkien's Linguistic Application of the Seventh Deadly Sin: Lust," *Mythlore* 26 nos. 3–4 (2008): 35. "Since Gollum is ravaged by the desire to possess the Ring, he condones lies, deceit, betrayal and even murder in the inventory of evil deeds he will commit in order to repossess it."

[7] Billy Graham, *The Seven Deadly Sins* (Grand Rapids: Zondervan, 1955), 106.

[8] Fairlie, 14. See also Livia Veselka, Erica A. Giammarco, and Philip A. Vernon, "The Dark Triad and the Seven Deadly Sins," *Personality and Individual Differences* 67 (2014): 78, which links greed with Machiavellianism and psychopathy. Greed can lead to a total lack of restraint in its abuse of other people.

[9] Fairlie, 89.

TABLE 5.4: SINS CONNECTED WITH GREED—OTHER SCRIPTURES

Reference	Verse	Sin
Psalm 10:3	The one greedy for gain curses and renounces the Lord (ESV).	cursing, forsaking God
Proverbs 15:27	Whoever is greedy for unjust gain troubles his own household, but he who hates bribes will live (ESV).	accepting bribes
Jeremiah 22:17	But thine eyes and thine heart are not but for thy covetousness, and for to shed innocent blood, and for oppression, and for violence, to do it.	murder, oppression, violence
Ezekiel 22:27	Her princes in the midst thereof are like wolves ravening the prey, to shed blood, and to destroy souls, to get dishonest gain.	
Micah 2:2	They covet fields, and take them by violence; and houses, and take them away: so they oppress a man and his house, even a man and his heritage.	
Ezekiel 22:12	In thee have they taken gifts to shed blood; thou hast taken usury and increase, and thou hast greedily gained of thy neighbours by extortion, and hast forgotten me, saith the Lord God.	accepting bribes, extortion
Ezekiel 33:31	For with their mouth they shew much love, but their heart goeth after their covetousness.	hypocrisy
Habakkuk 2:9	Woe to him that coveteth an evil covetousness to his house, that he may set his nest on high, that he may be delivered from the power of evil!	idolatry of security
Luke 16:13–14	No servant can serve two masters: for either he will hate the one, and love the other; or else he will hold to the one, and despise the other. Ye cannot serve God and mammon. And the Pharisees also, who were covetous, heard all these things: and they derided him.	idolatry of divided loyalty, mockery of truth

Reference	Verse	Sin
2 Peter 2:3	And through covetousness shall they with feigned words make merchandise of you.	lying, using people for profit

GREED TODAY

In our era, greed is a sanitized and respectable sin. Greed actually gained this respectability centuries ago. It has always been a favorite among the powerful in society. The pharaohs gilded their tombs with gold and built monuments to their own greatness. Alexander the Great wept when his greed for conquest outstripped the availability of lands to conquer. Even at the turn of the nineteenth century, Andrew Fuller lamented:

> It has long appeared to me that this species of covetousness will, in all probability, prove the eternal overthrow of more characters among professing people, than almost any other sin; and this because it is almost the only sin which may be indulged, and a profession of religion at the same time supported. If a man be a drunkard, a fornicator, an adulterer, or a liar; if he rob his neighbor, oppress the poor, or deal unjustly, he must give up his pretences to religion; or if not, his religious connexions, if they are worthy of being so denominated, will give him up: but he may *love the world, and the things of the world,* and at the same time retain his character.[10]

The problem has only increased since Fuller's day.

---

[10] Andrew Fuller, *The Backslider: His Nature, Symptoms, and Means for Recovery* (1801; repr., Birmingham: Solid Ground Christian Books, 2005), 28–29.

We prefer to distance ourselves from some forms of sin by feigning ignorance of the sinfulness of our behavior and its effects on others. Greed offers us a prime sin on which to experiment with this self-deception. We can explain away virtually every form of greed as an inescapable feature of our world situation. We can twist almost any form of greed into a virtue. John Cassian wrote that greed could always come up with "excellent and almost reasonable excuses" for its existence.[11]

Greed keeps the wheels of capitalism well-oiled and the machines of industry running smoothly. Without greed, stocks would plod along at an extremely modest pace. Without greed, we wouldn't have access to fifty kinds of cheese from fourteen countries. We wouldn't have entire stores overflowing with toys. We couldn't hype the latest technology with a smug and scornful attitude toward those whose electronics are antiquarian—they're six months old! Greed brings food from Tahiti to our dinner tables, krugerrands to our IRAs, and bigger screens to our home theaters. Have you ever looked at a house that was built prior to 1930? How much closet space did it have? Each room in a modern house boasts as much closet space as entire home had in the nineteenth century. We have to be able to store all of our stuff!

The church has been complicit in the growth of this culturally worshiped sin.

Greed drives us to work longer hours to buy bigger houses that cost more to air condition, insure, and maintain while we spend more time away from them in our offices trying to earn enough to pay for those houses. Greed propels us to gain disposable income

[11] Cassian, VII:7.

so that we can dispose of it—often unwisely. In some people, greed leads to hoarding. In others, it motivates spending. Greed cares not. It never has cared for the souls that it sucks every trace of decency and moderation out of.

No, we shouldn't seek a return to austerity by a self-righteous imitation of a bygone age, but when our storage units overflow with unworn clothes, unplayed games, unused tools, and unread books, we ought to question whether the conspicuous consumption of our twenty-first-century lives is really meeting the needs of our hearts. We ought to accept God's blessings without constantly demanding more. The church has been complicit in the growth of this culturally worshiped sin. When the church fails to distinguish between productivity (Prov. 10:4–5) and avarice or between prudent investment (Prov. 27:23–27) and greed, it encourages believers to follow their own feelings in pursuing wealth. Some plunge off the cliff into greed. Others plunge off the cliff into asceticism. Neither exhibits the proper love for God and others that the Bible requires.

Some of what we call progress is truly development. It genuinely improves life in imitation of our great Designer. But some "progress" is simply greed for anything new, faster, or more powerful as long as it promises to blunt our misery, distract us from tedium, and give us control over our destiny. We resist the web of greed not by throwing away the gifts of God, but by recognizing gifts as gifts, by making careful, thoughtful decisions about what we really need instead of glutting ourselves on whatever infatuates us today, and by studying contentment. Because greed is disordered love, the solution to greed is not self-willed contentment but the replacement of a bad love with a proper love. The psalmist thus prays, "Incline my heart unto thy testimonies, and not to covetousness"

(Ps. 119:36). Living life with an open hand—both to receive from the Lord and to give back to Him through sharing with others in need—helps us chasten our greedy desires and teaches us to love. By ordering our loves through growth in our knowledge of and obedience to Christ, we cut the strands of greed that captivate our hearts in its web.

6

GLUTTONY—
INSATIABLE APPETITES

> It is the great curse of gluttony that it ends by destroying
> all sense of the precious, the unique, the irreplaceable.[1]

Gluttony ranks lowest among the capital sins on the scale of its seeming destructiveness. We wonder why so many early Christians felt inclined to address a sin so petty that we would hardly even call it a sin today. Only a few scattered passages in Scripture address gluttony directly, and two of those (the only two occurrences of *phagos* φαγος and two of three occurrences of *oinopotēs* οινοποτης) were used by opponents of Jesus who were trying to impugn His character:

> The Son of man is come eating and drinking; and ye say,
> Behold a gluttonous man, and a winebibber, a friend of
> publicans and sinners! (Luke 7:34; cf. Matt. 11:19)

Christians in an earlier day recognized that gluttony threatens the traditional virtues of thrift and temperance. It really does abuse the good things that God has given to us. So maybe it has a place in the pantheon of serious sins after all.

DEFINING GLUTTONY

Gluttony is a disposition of the heart that is devoted to overindulging in food and drink as a significant (or *the* most significant)

---

[1] Dorothy Sayers, *The Whimsical Christian* (New York: Macmillan, 1978), 165.

source of pleasure in life. It turns enjoyment into an idol by making it both a directing force and an important goal in life. Gluttony magnifies the capacity of food and drink to bring gratification and amusement. A glutton lives to eat and drink. Such behavior grants illegitimate power and status to material things. Gluttony essentially glorifies as supremely valuable that part of the material world that can be consumed.

Gluttony takes several different forms. The most obvious form is excessive consumption. But can we automatically assume that obesity is a clear indication of gluttony while thinness is proof that a person has escaped from

> *Gluttony does not destroy love completely but distorts it.*

this sin? Sometimes a high metabolism, bulimia, or excessive devotion to exercise is the cause of a person's thinness. We ought not to congratulate ourselves that our escape from the external consequence of gluttony frees us from the snare of gluttony altogether. Remember that gluttony is a disposition of the heart that is devoted to overindulgence in food—an overindulgence that takes many forms. Gregory the Great used the fivefold expression "too soon, too delicately, too expensively, too greedily, too much" to express the ways in which we can overindulge in food.[2] The person who eats when he should be doing something else is being gluttonous. The picky person who turns up his nose at many foods in favor of only those foods that bring him the greatest comfort and pleasure is practicing gluttony. The connoisseur, who eats only cuisine that is finely prepared—the best of the best—is a glutton. The person who eats grossly, ignoring propriety and decency in the overwhelming urge to sate himself is acting as a glutton. So we

---

[2] Francine Prose, *Gluttony: The Seven Deadly Sins* (Oxford: Oxford University Press, 2003), 7.

must not be hasty to judge those who struggle with their weight, which may well have an explanation in a medical condition, while we excuse ourselves as innocent of this sin. Our attitude toward our food is important. If we elevate consumable goods to the status of a supreme good, we have fallen into gluttony.

We should enjoy the gifts that God has given us to enjoy. It certainly gives a father little delight to see his children ignoring his good gifts to them. But we shouldn't treat the gifts as though they had the ultimate power to please us. When we use the gifts of God immoderately, we're ascribing glory to the gift rather than to the Giver. This deifying of the natural world describes the philosophy of materialism. And if food and drink have supreme power to make us happy—if they are gods—then we can give ourselves over to them with abandon. This is precisely why gluttony "laughs at righteous restraint and scorns temperance and decency."[3]

Gluttony is one of the "warm" sins. It doesn't destroy love completely but distorts it. Sayers argues that gluttony is "the excess and perversion of that free, careless, and generous mood that desires to enjoy life and to see others enjoy it. But, like lust and wrath, it is a headless, heedless sin."[4] We cannot class it with the "cold" sins of envy, pride, and greed since gluttons tend to share their joy freely—too freely—with their fellowmen. The traditional picture of the glutton is a rotund but jolly sort of man, full of laughter and good cheer in the company of his friends, if a little short on self-control. This traditional image is incomplete because it omits the reality that gluttony is sin.

---

[3] Billy Graham, *The Seven Deadly Sins* (Grand Rapids: Zondervan Publishing House, 1955), 73.

[4] Sayers, 166.

KEY SCRIPTURE PASSAGES ON GLUTTONY

Several key biblical passages sharpen our understanding of the sin of gluttony in a way that helps us not to misidentify it. Almost in the middle of Deuteronomy, Moses describes an unusual sin warranting capital punishment. Over the space of four verses, the text treats a rebellious son whose disobedience is incorrigible. It then adds the paired qualities: "a glutton and a drunkard" (Deut. 21:20). The passage indicates that at least in this context gluttony is not an occasional or accidental overindulgence. It is a sustained prodigality that abuses the gifts of God, propriety, societal decency, and the clear command of God. Gluttony harms the glutton, his family, and society—and it doesn't do so primarily by causing obesity. It does harm through its wantonness. Gluttony involves shameless dissolution, out-of-control urges, and gross intemperance.

The second passage confirms this conclusion. Proverbs 23:20–21 warns, "Be not among winebibbers; among riotous eaters of flesh: for the drunkard and the glutton shall come to poverty: and drowsiness shall clothe a man with rags." The prodigal son provides a third example of the devastation produced by gluttony. Although Luke 15 doesn't use the word *gluttony*, it clearly

Gluttony encourages us to point fingers at others while excusing ourselves.

references "riotous living" (Luke 15:13). This word occurs in other passages such as Ephesians 5:18 ("not drunk with wine, wherein is **excess**"), Titus 1:6 ("having faithful children not accused of **riot**"), and 1 Peter 4:4 ("run not with them to the same excess of **riot**"). Each of these situations involves a loss of control and an abandonment of temperance.

We know that gluttony is not merely eating a little too much at one sitting since God ordained festivals for His people (*festival* is etymologically related to *feast*). On special occasions of celebration (Gen. 21:8; Esther 9:22), worship (Exod. 5:1), or honor (Esther 2:18; Luke 5:29) and in conjunction with hospitality (2 Sam. 3:20) and edification (Jude 1:12), the overabundance of food reflected the overabundance of joy. This is not the sin of gluttony, which cherishes greedy pleasure for its own sake. People who feast in the biblical sense eat at an appropriate time and place but in an "excessive" fashion because it is proper under the circumstances. In contrast, the glutton eats and drinks excessively out of a near-veneration of the eating experience.

INTERCONNECTIONS WITH OTHER SINS

Gluttony rests comfortably with other sins. In a fascinating passage that depicts the sins of Jerusalem through imagery, Isaiah 56:10 accuses the people of sloth, 56:11 treats greed, and 56:12 points to gluttony:

> All ye beasts of the field, come to devour, yea, all ye beasts in the forest. His watchmen are blind: they are all ignorant, they are all dumb dogs, they cannot bark; sleeping, lying down, loving to slumber. Yea, they are greedy dogs which can never have enough, and they are shepherds that cannot understand: they all look to their own way, every one for his gain, from his quarter. Come ye, say they, I will fetch wine, and we will fill ourselves with strong drink; and to morrow shall be as this day, and much more abundant. (Isa. 56:9–12)

The abuse of material blessings through the indiscriminate consumption of them is characteristic of those who don't know or serve the Lord. While vice lists tend to pair gluttony with the corresponding virtue of temperance, I would recommend that we add to temperance the virtue of stewardship. Stewardship knows that when the Master comes home, there is a great occasion for celebration. There will even be an intended and deliberate excess that corresponds to the joy of the occasion. This isn't gluttony. But stewardship also recognizes that "pulling out all the stops" all the time for the sake of pleasure squanders the Master's goods and weakens the capacities of His servants. We celebrate as a means to the end of bringing glory to God, not as an end in itself.

Gluttony tends to desolate. The individual locust eats a portion of a single plant. The plant recovers. Life goes on. A swarm of billions locusts devastates thousands of square miles, denuding every tree and devouring every green thing. Gluttony is that swarm. Its desolating character means that it must march onward, as the locusts must, to find more food. So gluttony simultaneously enervates the will and the capacity for proper work (tending toward sloth) while it demands new means of satiating its growing appetite. Gluttons waste their families' resources, leading to anger, bitterness, and conflict in the home. They lose their sense of productivity, leading to laziness and inactivity. Their addiction drives the need to acquire more money, even by illegitimate means; so the glutton faces a new temptation to lie, cheat, or steal enough to feed his habit. Paul illustrates this desolating character, idolatry, shamefulness, and materialism when he condemns false teachers "whose end is destruction, whose God is their belly, and whose glory is in their shame, who mind earthly things" (Phil. 3:19).

GLUTTONY TODAY

For much of the world's existence, gluttony was a sin reserved for the rich (except in the form of drunkenness, which was common among all classes). The ready availability of food, drink, and illicit drugs in the modern era has leveled that field. The proliferation of all-you-can-eat restaurants attests to the growth of this vice. So does the rise of gourmet restaurants that turn dinner into a "divine experience." They charge ghastly prices for entrance into these temples of food that is prepared by the high priests of gluttony and served up with the fanciest of names to indulge devoted worshipers. And who can forget the demand for finer, rarer, more expensive coffees or chocolates that we simply *must* have every day. Gluttony encourages us to point fingers at others while excusing ourselves. A certain jaded politician of the late twentieth century demanded that poor and middle-class Americans curb their excessive consumption of petroleum and energy while his own opulent houses consumed more energy than a small subdivision. And so the moderate glutton can always point a finger at those more gluttonous than himself.

We observed earlier that gluttons tend to share their joy freely. This makes them prime targets for the avaricious, who prey on the addictions and orgies of the glutton. The more devoted the glutton becomes to his gluttony, the more money the covetous man can make off of him by selling him food and drink. The major breweries in the Western world spend millions of dollars advertising their products to gluttons. And they do everything in their power to create more gluttons. They may put an appeal for moderation on their packaging ("Please drink responsibly"), but they desire nothing of the sort. If gluttons stopped guzzling, the avaricious would lose money. In the meantime, the glutton loses everything worth having in order to gain a very temporary pleasure. Sayers insightfully observed, "At length

> *When we eat, we must rejoice more in the Giver than the gift.*

[gluttony] issues in its own opposite—in that very dearth in the midst of plenty at which we stand horrified today."[5]

We must consider carefully whether we have corrupted a proper attitude toward eating and drinking, turning it from being a holy, thankful enjoyment of God's gifts into a selfish craving for pleasure. Repenting of our gluttony involves much more than reducing our caloric intake. Remember Gregory's axiom—"too soon, too delicately, too expensively, too greedily, too much." We eat in order to live, but we do not exist for the sake of eating. Finding ourselves yearning for a particular food, particular quality of food, or particular food experience as the high point of our day is dangerous. This has twisted pleasure into a god worthy of our devotion. And, yes, food really does control the thoughts of many of us.

Using food as a means of escape—whether from boredom, from misery, from studies, or from labor—indicates the rise of gluttony in our hearts. In this regard, gluttony is readily identifiable with one of its subsidiary sins, drunkenness. When we eat, we must rejoice more in the Giver than the gift. While we appreciate the flavors, we direct honor for wisdom and kindness to the Giver, not to the food. We are careful not to overeat, but we are also careful not to venerate the eating experience. When we recognize our role as stewards of God's gifts and eat and drink for His glory (1 Cor. 10:31) instead of living as endpoint consumers, then God's Word transforms our thinking. And the effect of this transformation reaches well beyond our waistlines. Since gluttony often stems from pride, sloth, selfishness, rebelliousness, or idolatry and since it leads to the same sins as well as to anger, lust, and lying, learning to be stewards of our consumption will help transform our attitude toward these connected sins.

---

[5] Sayers, 166.

7

LUST—
CORRUPTED LOVE

> Of the seven deadly sins, Lust is the only one about
> which all mankind (with very few exceptions) knows
> something from experience.[1]

Whlie the author of this quotation is simultaneously too pessi-
mistic (lust is not as absolutely controlling as he assumes) and too
optimistic (pride, anger, and even sloth are sins we have all probably experienced), his sense of the near universality of this sin hits
close to the mark. If we could put one sin to death with a magic
bullet, lust would receive many votes to be that sin. We read verses
such as, "This you know with certainty, that no immoral or impure
person or covetous man, who is an idolater, has an inheritance in
the kingdom of Christ and God" (Eph. 5:5, NASB), and, "Do you
not know that the unrighteous will not inherit the kingdom of
God? Do not be deceived; neither fornicators, nor idolaters, nor
adulterers, nor effeminate, nor homosexuals, nor thieves, nor the
covetous, nor drunkards, nor revilers, nor swindlers, will inherit
the kingdom of God" (1 Cor. 6:9–10, NASB), and we are shocked
at the eternal effects of our sin. We feel the profound weight of
condemnation these verses lay on us. The fact that Paul reminds
his readers, "Such were some of you: but ye are washed, but ye
are sanctified, but ye are justified in the name of the Lord Jesus,
and by the Spirit of our God" (6:11), doesn't alleviate the pangs of

---

[1] Christopher Sykes, "On Lust," in Ian Fleming, *The Seven Deadly Sins* (New York:
William Morrow and Company, 1962), 67.

conscience and the sting of guilt for those who struggle with the capital sin of lust.

Our concern here, however, is to develop the interconnections of this sin with other sins in order to understand better its source sins and consequent sins. One of the problems that we face in responding to our lust is the fact that this intense desire seems to "come out of nowhere" and strike us when we are ill-prepared to deal with it. We don't recognize how lust arises in the first place; so we aren't alert to its entrapment until it's too late.

DEFINING LUST

A discussion of lust leaves room for misunderstanding. In English, the term *lust* fills a spectrum from broad to narrow definition. Broadly, lust is any type of desire. More narrowly, lust is any type of sinful desire. In fact, the Bible uses the term most frequently in this generic sense of sinful desire. But in the narrower context of the capital sins, *lust* refers to the sinful desire for sensual experience outside of marriage as defined in Scripture.

Lust is a corrupted form of love for others that has turned inward on itself. This means, at the very least, that lust cannot exist apart from underlying pride. God designed us to appreciate beauty, to relate to each other socially, and to desire such relationships. He also planned for His image-bearers to express this combined appreciation and desire in a heightened, unique, monogamous, heterosexual covenant relationship to which He added physical pleasure as means of sealing and blessing that relationship. He planned to intensify our love for a spouse, magnify our appreciation of beauty, and strengthen our commitment to this covenant relationship through physical pleasure. That physical pleasure was originally a sign, seal, and result of the relationship. God didn't originally create it to exist apart from that relationship. The Fall corrupted our hearts and minds so that now we instinctively care less about God and others than about our own physical pleasure.[2] We circumvent God's method of providing pleasure (the unique, monogamous, heterosexual covenant relationship) and come to view God's plan as insignificant in comparison to physical pleasure. Instead of loving another person and expressing that love through the physical relationship, we're born loving ourselves and seeking to experience pleasure in and for ourselves regardless of how we obtain that pleasure. In our fallen state, the experience of pleasure readily becomes a god to us—receiving the worship we owe God alone and commanding our allegiance.[3]

Lust overlaps the capital sins of greed and gluttony most closely. Like greed, lust frequently wants to acquire something. Instead of pursuing money, lust pursues people for the sexual pleasure they can provide. Lust creates a distorted perspective in

> *Lust is a corrupted form of love for others that has turned inward on itself.*

which people exist less as distinct beings made in God's image than as objects for one's personal gratification. Greed seeks the acquisition of more things, but it often fails to use or enjoy the things that

---

[2] "Lust is an idolatrous and ultimately insatiable desire that rejects God's rule and seeks satisfaction apart from Him. God says, 'You shall not covet' (Exodus 20:17). But lust tells us that what we don't have is exactly what we need. Lust covets the forbidden. Lust grasps for, with our eyes, hearts, imaginations, or bodies, what God has said no to." Joshua Harris, *Not Even a Hint* (Sisters, OR: Multnomah, 2003), 38–39.

[3] Kathleen McGowan, "Seven Deadly Sins," *Discover,* September 2009, http://discovermagazine.com/2009/sep/05-i-didnt-sin-it-was-my-brain. "When it comes to lust, neuroimaging confirms that the prurient urge is all-encompassing." McGowan observes that at least three separate portions of the brain activate when a person views pornography. Lust triggers the brain's reward centers—strengthening and encouraging the participant in this sin to go back to it for more.

it acquires; greed finds pleasure only in the acquisition itself. There is a type of lust that is exclusively greedy (as there is a type of lust that is cruel and savage), but most lust is different from greed in its desire to experience pleasure through a relationship—however fleeting it may be. So lust is similar to gluttony in its desire to experience pleasure. The church fathers considered lust to be a "warm" sin because it misuses (rather than rejects) the love and pleasure that God created.

Our experience with lust is very roughly analogous to a child's attitude toward an inheritance. Legally, the child possesses his inheritance as a sign, seal, and result of his standing in relation to his parents. The inheritance is a blessing that should strengthen the bond between parent and child since it is a reflection of the parents' desire for the good of the child. But we all know grasping, selfish children who care nothing for their parents and who secretly hope for their soon demise so that the children can seize the inheritance.[4] We know that something is seriously wrong with those who despise the relationship with their parents and who care only about the pleasures that they might greedily acquire. that's the way lust is. It masquerades as love, but it's really veiled selfishness. It's "an abusive and manipulative attitude toward persons . . . ; treating them as objects or pawns."[5]

Ultimately, lust destroys all who succumb to it. God made us to appreciate beauty; instead we mar it. He created us to desire constructive relationships; instead we tear them apart by our self-love. As Karl Olsson observes, "Unlike good love, lust ultimately

---

[4] The prodigal son comes to mind as an example of a greedy child who was more concerned about pleasure than about his relationship with his father (Luke 15:11–13).

[5] Donald Capps and Melissa Haupt, "The Deadly Sins: How They Are Viewed and Experienced Today," *Pastoral Psychology* 60 (2011): 794.

isolates; it destroys rather than nourishes the life union. And it does this because, perversely, it confuses means and ends. In lusting for the other, I really love myself. The other becomes an instrument of my satisfaction: a bright plaything which finally grows shabby and unwanted."[6] The object of lust suffers the humiliation of being treated as an object rather than as a person, and the one who lusts suffers the dehumanizing effects of pursuing self-love and pleasure in the place of love for God and others (Prov. 6:32). Lust is thus cruel to all parties involved.

If we combine these components, we understand lust to be a corrupted self-love that seeks to experience pleasure through the contemplation and use of people as objects of physical gratification.[7]

KEY SCRIPTURE PASSAGES ON LUST

Since pride, envy, greed, and sloth are direct antitheses to the virtues of humility, contentment, and faith/faithfulness, the Bible castigates rather than regulates these sins. But since wrath, gluttony, and lust warp the virtues of justice, joy, and love without always totally destroying these virtues, God helps His people understand His boundaries and standards in regard to the abuse of virtue. He doesn't repudiate the good that He has created—it aligns with His own character—so He regulates our understanding of that good in order to prevent our corrupting it through misuse. The desire for pleasure is one such "good" that God has created. The consequence of this truth is that Scripture rarely addresses lust as lust. Rather, it teaches that adultery (Lev. 18:20), bestiality (Exod.

---

[6] Karl Olsson, *Seven Sins and Seven Virtues* (New York: Harper & Brothers, 1959), 54.

[7] There are forms of lust that are so debased that they move beyond the sensual contemplation and use of "people" to the sensual contemplation and use of "other beings and objects," but these specific sins are typically the result of unrepented lust as defined above.

22:19), sodomy (Lev. 18:22; 20:13), rape (Deut. 22:25), polygamy (implied by Matt. 19:5; Eph. 5:31), prostitution (Lev. 19:29), and incest (Lev. 18:17; 20:12, 14, 20, 21) are violations of both God's law and His design for human fulfillment.[8] The monastic orders of the early church and later the Roman Catholic Church failed to make this distinction. They assumed that physical pleasure must always be wrong, and they sought to silence their own passions through a total renunciation of physical pleasure, even in marriage. Such attitudes are indefensible in light of Scripture (see especially Song of Solomon).

Jesus indicates that lust is a mental state of desire that precedes an outward action, "I say unto you, That whosoever looketh on a woman to lust after her hath committed adultery with her already in his heart" (Matt. 5:28). This passage requires fidelity in heart as well as in behavior. The people of

> *The Fall corrupted our hearts and minds so that now we instinctively care less about God and others than about our own physical pleasure.*

God must exhibit perfect faithfulness and purity. Failure in the area of lust is not benign. It has lasting consequences. The life of Samson demonstrates the seriousness of a lustful disposition. After a brief mention of his birth in Judges 13, Samson's story takes up the next three chapters (14–16). The very first verse that pertains to Samson's adult life demonstrates that he was a man characterized by lust:

> Samson went down to Timnath, and saw a woman in Timnath of the daughters of the Philistines. . . . Samson

---

[8] There are, of course, numerous passages of Scripture that forbid the individual sexual sins, but the intent in this book is to show how lust interconnects with other sins.

said unto his father, Get her for me; for she pleaseth me well. (Judg. 14:1, 3)

Samson had no concern for God's reputation or commands, for the purity of Israel, or for propriety. He had no respect for his parents. He saw, desired, and demanded to fulfill that desire. Lest we think that Samson was simply marrying outside his family but without further character defect, the Bible indicates that this was a habitual problem with lust since we find him with a prostitute later on: "Then went Samson to Gaza, and saw there an harlot, and went in unto her" (Judg. 16:1).

Finally, he pursued a third Philistine woman, Delilah, to his own destruction. (Judg. 16:4) Samson's life was out of control because he was ruled by his sensual desires. We know about his physical strength, but we also grieve his folly. He leapt from one crisis to another, every one of them a product of his lust. In spite of his faith in God, sins multiplied in his life because he wouldn't control his lust.

Another biblical figure exhibits an even greater fall from glory. Solomon was the wisest man in the ancient world, but he proved to be a fool in several crucial areas of life. Solomon's folly derived largely from lust. His wisdom crumbled when his pursuit of sensual pleasure undermined his decision-making and his faithfulness to God. His lust brought devastating consequences to his personal legacy, to his dynasty, and to the entire nation.

King Solomon loved many strange women, together with the daughter of Pharaoh, women of the Moabites, Ammonites, Edomites, Zidonians, and Hittites; of the nations concerning which the Lord said unto the children of

Israel, Ye shall not go in to them, neither shall they come in unto you: for surely they will turn away your heart after their gods: Solomon clave unto these in love. And he had seven hundred wives, princesses, and three hundred concubines: and his wives turned away his heart. For it came to pass, when Solomon was old, that his wives turned away his heart after other gods: and his heart was not perfect with the Lord his God, as was the heart of David his father. (1 Kings 11:1–4)

In interacting with the Pharisees, Jesus gave insight into the sin of lust. While many sins are visible because they occur in outward actions toward others, underlying motivations and desires drive those sins. In a list of these underlying motivations, Jesus included three that relate to lust.

That which cometh out of the man, that defileth the man. For from within, out of the heart of men, proceed evil thoughts, adulteries, fornications, murders, thefts, covetousness, wickedness, deceit, lasciviousness [sensuality], an evil eye, blasphemy, pride, foolishness: all these evil things come from within, and defile the man. (Mark 7:20–23)

So while we can readily recognize the actions that proceed from lust (this passage mentions adultery, fornication, and sensuality), these actions spring from something intangible that is occurring in the heart. Interestingly, the Bible often doesn't separate greed, lust, and gluttony from each other in terms of the underlying disposition. Instead, it encompasses all three under the general heading of lust.[9] The corruption of our hearts' desires so that we turn

---

[9] A notable exception occurs in 1 John 2:15–16 where "lust of the flesh" seems to include sexual lust and gluttony while "lust of the eyes" refers to greed.

away from God and seek our good and our pleasure outside of His plans for us is lust. We're disposed to contrive our own pleasure instead of relying on God and His will for that pleasure. And in this disposition, our hearts devise alternative means to satisfy our longings. These alternatives are the individual acts of sin that Jesus addresses in Mark 7.

INTERCONNECTIONS WITH OTHER SINS

Joseph provides a positive Old Testament example of a man who refused to succumb to lust but fled from it instead. In the process of his resistance, Joseph indicated that immorality with Potiphar's wife would actually have been at least a threefold offense, involving adultery, betrayal of his master, and godlessness.

> But he refused and said to his master's wife, "Behold, because of me my master has no concern about anything in the house, and he has put everything that he has in my charge. He is not greater in this house than I am, nor has he kept back anything from me except you, because you are his wife. How then can I do this great wickedness and sin against God?" (Gen. 39:8–9, ESV)

Joseph understood that sins are interconnected. The ostensibly isolated sin of adultery is not one sin but many. And so it is with all lust. The desire for self-serving pleasure in defiance of God's plan always attaches to other sins. Some sins cause lust while others result from it, but lust is simply part of the terrible web of attendant sins—all of which are dragging us down to destruction.

Solomon's wisdom crumbled when his pursuit of sensual pleasure undermined his faithfulness to God.

Some sins frequently lead to lust. The most prominent of these is sloth. Remember David's example in 2 Samuel 11. When we experience boredom or discouragement in life that no longer recognizes the good that God is doing, we begin to look for good outside of His plan. A girl who is single might become discouraged when she sees all of her friends pairing off and marrying. Her mind begins to question God's goodness toward her and to doubt His care. This discouragement may erode her sense of being worthy of love and attention—leaving only mind-numbing "experiences" to fill the void of her hurt. The middle-aged man may become bored with the routine of his relationship with his wife. He demands a greater thrill and pleasure out of a life that is rushing through his fingers. McCracken concurs, "People turn to lust because of ennui, boredom, dissatisfaction, their inability to make constructive use of leisure. From it they hope for excitement, adventure, or in the case of the middle-aged, one last fling! It is resorted to as an antidote to the flatness of existence, a means of filling the vacuum in their inner life."[10] And Sayers observes that sloth is "the child of covetousness and the parent of those other two sins . . . lust and gluttony."[11] Doubt and despair are such dark adversaries that we long to silence them through pleasure, and one of the most visceral pleasures that can distract us is lust.

William Stafford believes that lust can arise from five of the other capital sins. "Lust carries with it an even more serous spiritual disease: that of pride. In the field of sexual life, he himself has displaced God. So it is with all the other deadly sins, which often wash up in the wake of lust. Avarice can accumulate 'sex objects' as personal possessions, while anger can use sex to dominate or

---

[10] Robert J. McCracken, *What Is Sin? What Is Virtue?* (New York: Harper & Row, 1966), 48–49.

[11] Dorothy Sayers, *The Whimsical Christian* (New York: Macmillan, 1978), 155.

batter or avenge. Envy can sprout out of unappeased sexual long-ing, when someone else wins the love you crave. *Accidie*—sloth, despair—can demoralize us into being someone else's toy."[12]

A closer look at the biblical example of Samson reveals how many different sins attended or resulted from his lust (Table 7.1).

TABLE 7.1: SINS CONNECTED WITH LUST—THE LIFE OF SAMSON

Judges	Verse	Sin
14:2	I have seen a woman in Timnath of the daughters of the Philistines: now therefore get her for me to wife.	disobeying God
16:4	And it came to pass afterward, that he loved a woman in the valley of Sorek, whose name was Delilah.	
14:3	Then his father and his mother said unto him, Is there never a woman among the daughters of thy brethren, or among all my people, that thou goest to take a wife of the uncircumcised Philistines? And Samson said unto his father, Get her for me.	dishonoring parents
14:8–9	And after a time he returned to take her, and he turned aside to see the carcase of the lion: and, behold, there was a swarm of bees and honey in the carcase of the lion. And he took thereof in his hands, and went on eating, and came to his father and mother, and he gave them, and they did eat: but he told not them that he had taken the honey out of the carcase of the lion.	breaking vows, deceit

---

[12] William S. Stafford, *Disordered Loves: Healing the Seven Deadly Sins* (Boston: Cowley Publications, 1994), 48.

Judges	Verse	Sin
14:10–12	Samson made there a feast; for so used the young men to do. And it came to pass, when they saw him, that they brought thirty companions to be with him. And Samson said unto them, I will now put forth a riddle unto you.	revelry, gluttony
14:19	And he went down to Ashkelon, and slew thirty men of them, and took their spoil, and gave change of garments unto them which expounded the riddle.	murder, injustice
15:3–5	And Samson said concerning them, Now shall I be more blameless than the Philistines, though I do them a displeasure. And Samson went and caught three hundred foxes, and took firebrands, and turned tail to tail, and put a firebrand in the midst between two tails. And when he had set the brands on fire, he let them go into the standing corn of the Philistines, and burnt up both the shocks, and also the standing corn, with the vineyards and olives.	vandalism, wanton destruction
15:7	And Samson said unto them, Though ye have done this, yet will I be avenged of you, and after that I will cease.	anger, revenge
16:1	Then went Samson to Gaza, and saw there an harlot, and went in unto her.	fornication
16:10 (cf. 16:13, 15)	And Delilah said unto Samson, Behold, thou hast mocked me, and told me lies: now tell me, I pray thee, wherewith thou mightest be bound.	lying

Judges	Verse	Sin
16:16–17	And it came to pass, when she pressed him daily with her words, and urged him, so that his soul was vexed unto death; that he told her all his heart, and said unto her, There hath not come a razor upon mine head; for I have been a Nazarite unto God from my mother's womb: if I be shaven, then my strength will go from me, and I shall become weak, and be like any other man.	spiritual insensibleness, gullibility
16:20	And she said, The Philistines be upon thee, Samson. And he awoke out of his sleep, and said, I will go out as at other times before, and shake myself. And he wist not that the Lord was departed from him.	
16:28	And Samson called unto the Lord, and said, O Lord God, remember me, I pray thee, and strengthen me, I pray thee, only this once, O God, that I may be at once avenged of the Philistines for my two eyes.	self-centered revenge

The other examples of lust in Scripture—from the men of Sodom in Genesis 19 to Shechem in Genesis 34, to Judah in Genesis 38, and on through the Benjamites in Judges 19 to David in 2 Samuel 11—demonstrate that lust virtually never stands alone. It's motivated by and motivates pride, disobedience, selfishness, violence, insolence, indifference, and revenge. Like all of the other sins we've explored, lust is part of a great web of iniquity whose inception and culmination are difficult to pinpoint and whose strands are difficult to cut.

LUST TODAY

One of the great concerns that the church faces in our era is the way lust has brought about the precipitous fall of some pastors, teachers, counselors, and longstanding believers. Our world uses sensuality as one of the quickest avenues to pleasure. It also uses sensuality to sell products, to manipulate attitudes, and to control minds. On the one hand, music, movies, and magazines—including online versions of all of these—glorify lust as the supreme good. On the other hand, society recoils in mock horror at the consequences of this glorification of lust. This sin grips the lowest criminal and the highest star. It extends through sports figures, politicians, actors, musicians, business people, and clergy. Everyone wants pleasure. Everyone longs to escape pain, misery, and boredom. And lust offers a quick but inglorious way to gain this pleasure.[13]

Since one of the primary sins that leads to a weakening of mind and heart in discouragement is sloth, we have to be on guard against this despondency. While some slothful individuals are totally inert, many others try to silence the agony of their hearts through pleasure. Sloth encourages us to give up on God because we feel that He has given up on us (or that He doesn't exist at all). This feeling of profound loss leads to a hopelessness that quits in the Christian life. Sloth undermines faithfulness. It stops fighting. It sees no point in continuing the long war against sin since it sees no good outcome in sight. And through this process of thinking, sloth paves the way for lust. Sloth also increases the opportunity for lustful thoughts to take possession of an idle mind, just as it did in David's life. As children of our Father, we must recognize when such discouragement is preying on our minds. Lest we fall away from Him, God urges us to seek the encouragement of pastors and friends who will point us to the truth that we cannot see for ourselves (James 5:14–18).

---

[13] Laurie Hall presents the suffering that stems from this sin in *An Affair of the Mind: One Woman's Courageous Battle to Salvage Her Family from the Devastation of Pornography* (Colorado Springs: Focus on the Family, 1996). She details the addictive quality of lust due to the pleasure associated with this sin, but she also shows the terrible consequences that result from such an addiction.

Pride nourishes lust because pride exalts a person in his own thinking to the point he believes that he deserves pleasure on his own terms. This diminishes the sinfulness of lust in his estimation. Pride also seduces a person into thinking that he can get away with lust even if it is sinful. It acts like a narcotic that dulls our thinking and that hides reality from us. Rebecca DeYoung observed this tendency when she produced a short list of famous figures who wandered into lust through the path of pride: "Riding the horse of vainglorious fame leads many to fall into the pigpen of lust and shame."[14]

If people of great faith can succumb to this sin as Samson and David did, we must take care to discern the roads by which our own hearts lead us to lust. Our selfishness, pride, sloth, envy, wrath, greedy, or gluttony in other areas of life will increase the probability of a reckless and precipitous fall into lust. And so in the process of our God-ordained pursuit of sanctification, we must treat our sin as both individual (recognizing the specific tendencies in our own hearts) and interrelated (recognizing how our sins connect with and feed on each other).

> *Pride nourishes lust because pride exalts a person in his own thinking to the point he believes that he deserves pleasure on his own terms.*

[14] Rebecca Konyndyk DeYoung, *Vainglory: The Forgotten Vice* (Grand Rapids: Eerdmans, 2014), 93. DeYoung lists Bill Clinton, Tiger Woods, John Edwards, Ben Rothlisburger, and David Petraeus among the examples from the early twenty-first century.

8

WRATH—
IMPLACABLE ANGER

> Anger is intensely personal. It is the quintessential individual signature emotion: I am what makes me mad.[1]

Anger is a fierce, destructive response to causes such as offended justice, actual hurt or the threat of hurt, and frustration.[2] If our sense of justice were perfect, then our anger would always be appropriate. But our anger tends to get out of hand. Why?

Four Reasons for Uncontrolled Anger

First, our sense of justice is warped. Because of our fallen condition, we don't think clearly about what justice and injustice really are. If I hit too many red lights in a row, I get angry because I feel that I ought to hit more green lights than red. If someone else gets a raise and I don't, I get angry because I feel that I work at least as hard as the next person. If the referees call my team for twelve more fouls than the opposing team, I get angry because I think fouls ought to even out. If a neighbor's pets are running loose, I get angry because he's destroying my property in the selfish attempt to preserve his own (or maybe worse, out of a careless indifference toward everyone else around him). If someone calls me a name, I get angry because I feel that he's trying to win friends by attacking me.

---

[1] Rick Ezell, *The Seven Sins of Highly Defective People* (Grand Rapids: Kregel, 2003), 53.

[2] See Aristotle, *Rhetoric,* II.2–3 for a development of the causes of anger and our response to these causes.

Selfishness sees many issues as matters of justice that have nothing to do with justice at all. There's no law of the universe that requires you to hit 75 percent green lights, or even 50 percent. There's no

Wrath will not wait patiently for God's timing in the execution of justice.

law that requires employers to distribute pay exactly equally.[3] There's no law that urges basketball officials to maintain an equal number of trips to the charity stripe for each team. Anger prevents us from considering alternative reasons for another person's behavior because it jumps to conclusions concerning the justness of a situation. Maybe our team was more aggressive. Maybe your neighbor's dogs are running loose because a thief who broke into his house left the gate open. Maybe that driver is weaving in traffic because he's having a heart attack or seizure. If we're willing to consider the causes of our anger, we might begin to recognize the selfishness, pride, and cruelty in our anger-inspired desire for revenge. This is a step in the biblical direction of relinquishing almost all of our anger to God. Let Him judge. He knows all the facts. He's keenly aware of genuine wrongs committed. And He is committed to justice.

Second, we sin when we wield anger too fiercely. Righteous anger seeks no more than justice. But I think we can all admit from experience that that isn't how anger works. We want a pound of flesh in return for an ounce of offense. Doesn't this sound a lot

---

[3] The reverse can also be true. In one of Jesus' parables, a householder hired workers in the early morning as well as at the third, sixth, ninth, and eleventh hours of the day. When the householder paid each of the workers the same wage, the ones who had worked all day murmured angrily against the householder for the perceived injustice. They believed in equal work for equal pay, but they didn't believe in equal pay for unequal work. When their sense of justice was violated, they responded in hostility toward the householder even though he had done them no wrong.

like Lamech in Genesis 4? "Lamech said unto his wives, Adah and Zillah, Hear my voice; ye wives of Lamech, hearken unto my speech: for I have slain a man to my wounding, and a young man to my hurt. If Cain shall be avenged sevenfold, truly Lamech seventy and sevenfold" (Gen. 4:23–24). His anger is utterly out of proportion to justice. We don't kill people for small infractions or personal insults. Or do we? We might not use a physical weapon, but many of us have engaged in one form of character assassination or another in response to a slight or insult. We blog about the offense in an attempt to exact revenge even if our adversary offended us accidentally, even if that adversary doesn't know that he did wrong, and even if the wrong was trivial.

Third, we sin by holding our anger too long. God indicates that even righteous anger has an expiration date for humans. "Be ye angry, and sin not: let not the sun go down upon your wrath" (Eph. 4:26). We simply cannot hold even justifiable anger in our hearts without being corrupted by the emotion itself. Anger destroys. When we direct it against a genuine injustice or a genuine threat, that destructive power protects justice and saves lives. But anger is a lot like dynamite. Expended correctly at the proper target, in the proper measure, and at the proper time, it destroys exactly what should be destroyed. But, like dynamite, if we keep it around, it "sweats," or becomes increasingly unstable in our lives, and it makes us edgy and prone to destroy what is good.[4] This happens to many believers who correctly identify and grieve the wickedness of a surrounding culture but who do not relinquish to God

---

[4] When dynamite is stored for a long period of time, nitroglycerin will begin to seep out of the stabilizing base of absorbent clay, sawdust, or diatomaceous earth that it's suspended in. This process is known as "sweating," and it returns the nitroglycerin to its highly unstable form that's likely to explode with the least jostling.

the right to judge. Their anger might have been justly spawned, but if left to fester, it destroys those who are angry.

Fourth, we can sin by failing to be angry when anger is appropriate. This counterintuitive response typically involves the sin of sloth, which we addressed earlier. When we give up in the face of evil that seems too extensive or too powerful to combat, we're failing to use anger as God intends. We don't cede this world to our Adversary. We don't yield our hearts to his malicious control. We wield the weapons of spiritual warfare (not physical unless called by a legitimate civil authority to do so) in appropriate anger against the evil that pervades and surrounds us.

> *Counterintuitively, we can sin by failing to be angry when anger is appropriate. This response typically involves the sin of sloth.*

DEFINING WRATH

Wrath, as a capital sin, expresses the entrenched disposition of anger. In this context, *wrath* isn't referring to the settled character trait that God possesses and wields righteously on the basis of His perfect execution of justice. Since anger has a legitimate role in a believer's life, God doesn't prohibit it completely. He regulates it in a fashion designed to keep it from turning into the capital sin of wrath. Justifiable anger is a measured, just response to an offense against actual justice as defined by God. Anger can be controlled. The vice of wrath is uncontrolled. In terms of the capital sin, wrath is the disposition that wields excessive or unjustified, fierce, destructive force against a person or object in response to either a sense of offended justice or an experience of hurt or frustration.[5]

---

[5] W. H. Auden adds this helpful clarification on the origin of anger, "Natural anger is a reflex reaction, not a voluntary one; it is a response to a real situation of threat

An interesting story in the book of Judges demonstrates how quickly anger can get out of hand. Gideon had just obeyed the Lord in leading three hundred men against the Midianite hordes. *After* the initial victory Gideon called for the men of Ephraim (whom he had not invited to participate in the battle) to seize the fords of the Jordan River to keep the scattered Midianites from escaping. Though they complied, the soldiers of Ephraim were angry:

> The men of Ephraim said unto him, Why hast thou served us thus, that thou calledst us not, when thou wentest to fight with the Midianites? And they did chide with him sharply. And he said unto them, What have I done now in comparison of you? Is not the gleaning of the grapes of Ephraim better than the vintage of Abiezer? God hath delivered into your hands the princes of Midian, Oreb and Zeeb: and what was I able to do in comparison of you? Then their anger was abated toward him, when he had said that. (Judg. 8:1–3)

Notice that their anger derived from a perceived injustice, namely, their feeling that Gideon should have included them in the initial battle. Questions would naturally arise for the Ephramites: (1) Was Gideon trying to set himself up as king, and he left us out?

---

and danger, and as soon as the threat is removed, the anger subsides." "On Anger," in Fleming, *The Seven Deadly Sins*, 79. When the anger Auden refers to becomes systemic or sustained, it has become the capital sin of wrath.

June Hunt defines anger as "a strong emotion of irritation, agitation, or hostility that occurs when a need or expectation is not met. Actually, anger is a secondary response to something else—it's an upsetting emotional reaction to an assumed 'right' that has been violated or not fulfilled." *Keeping Your Cool When Your Anger Is Hot: Practical Steps to Temper Fiery Emotions* (Eugene, OR: Harvest House Publishers, 2009), 24. Garrett Keizer notes, "Anger is often nothing more than a hasty judgment registered as a nasty emotion." *The Enigma of Anger: Essays on a Sometimes Deadly Sin* (San Francisco: Jossey-Bass, 2002), 325.

(2) Isn't this a deliberate insult to treat us like pawns and under-lings? (3) Was Gideon trying to get all the spoils for himself, and he only called us when the enemy escaped? Ultimately, Gideon had done no wrong. He committed no injustice. He hadn't insulted Ephraim. The Ephraimites were struggling with their own tribal pride that warped their perception of the situation into seeing it as an affront and insult. Wrath is this underlying disposition that al-lows any perception of injustice to flare into open hostility. Wrath rarely checks the facts and asks reasonable questions. It is spoiling for a fight—frequently motivated by pride, envy, greed, or lust.

Sometimes wrath is a response to an injury or wounding. Lamech's words in Genesis 4:23–24 don't indicate that he was acting in pur-suit of justice. His pride was wounded, and that wounded pride lashed out in violent, dispro-portional wrath. Physical

If we allow anger to become our prevailing disposition, it becomes the sin of wrath.

and emotional pain can lead to anger as Bildad's response to Job indicates: "You who tear yourself in your anger, shall the earth be forsaken for you, or the rock be removed out of its place?" (Job 18:4, ESV).

We all experience genuine injustice, perceived injustice, hurt, and frustration throughout our lives. Anger is the emotion that prepares us to respond to these situations with an energetic, self-preserving fight-or-flight reaction. But if we allow anger to become our prevailing disposition, it becomes the sin of wrath, which encourages us to overreact to the suffering of life in a man-ner that tries to destroy all causes for suffering. Wrath will not submit to God's wisdom and sovereign control over suffering and frustration in this world. Wrath will not wait patiently for God's timing in the execution of justice. So ultimately, the human vice of wrath is insubordination to God.

Key Scripture Passages on Wrath

The book of Esther provides important confirmation of the accuracy of the definition of *wrath* stated earlier in this chapter. First, these passages establish that wrath often proceeds from a sense of violated justice. When Queen Vashti chose to disobey the king's command, she was seen as questioning his authority. This offense fueled the king's wrath.

> But the queen Vashti refused to come at the king's commandment by his chamberlains: therefore was the king very wroth, and his anger burned in him. (Esther 1:12)

When Mordecai refused to prostrate himself before Haman, he provoked Haman's wrath. While Haman's pride obviously played a significant part in his wrathful response, we shouldn't overlook the fact that Haman held great authority in the kingdom. In a purely secular sense he "deserved" the honor and admiration of the people of the land, and when he didn't receive it from Mordecai, his sense of justice was violated. True, his sense of justice was corrupted by his own pride, but this sense of justice had some basis in the position that he held in the royal court.

> When Haman saw that Mordecai bowed not, nor did him reverence, then was Haman full of wrath. (Esther 3:5)

When Queen Esther exposed Haman's plot to exterminate the Jews, King Ahasuerus exploded in wrath. The fact that Haman's following behavior appeared to be assaulting the queen sealed his fate. Injustice kindled wrath in the person whose rights were being attacked.

> The king arising from the banquet of wine in his wrath went into the palace garden: and Haman stood up to make request for his life to Esther the queen; for he saw that there was evil determined against him by the king. Then the king returned out of the palace garden into the place of the banquet of wine; and Haman was fallen upon the bed whereon Esther was. Then said the king, Will he force the queen also before me in the house? . . . So they hanged Haman on the gallows that he had prepared for Mordecai. Then was the king's wrath pacified. (Esther 7:7–8, 10)

Second, wrath tends to wield excessive or unjustified, fierce, destructive force against a person or object that has offended one's sense of justice. Vashti's behavior seemed to be a threat to the entire legal code of the Persians; so Ahasuerus responded to Vashti's disobedience by stripping her of her position as queen (Esther 1:21–22). Haman responded to Mordecai's affront—an offense that wounded Haman's pride—by plotting the annihilation of all the Jews. His behavior exemplifies our tendency to direct wrath away from the one who actually hurt us and toward innocent bystanders.

> He thought scorn to lay hands on Mordecai alone; for they had shewed him the people of Mordecai: wherefore Haman sought to destroy all the Jews that were throughout the whole kingdom of Ahasuerus, even the people of Mordecai. (Esther 3:6)

Haman's behavior cannot be construed as just. Even if Mordecai had been wrong in his actions, the Jews as a race didn't deserve such retaliation. Although it ostensibly undergirds justice, wrath frequently undermines it. Simeon and Levi demonstrate this in Genesis 34. When Shechem assaulted their sister (though he actually loved her, he showed it in a sinful, uncontrolled way), Simeon and Levi conspired to destroy the entire city. They slaughtered all the men, stole all the property, and enslaved all the women (presumably to serve their own lust). It's hard to conceive how one man's sinful behavior warranted the vile and cruel behavior perpetrated against all of his relations and people. But such is wrath. It distorts reality and makes a mockery of justice. In lashing out against an injustice that might have occurred sometime somewhere, wrath often destroys the innocent.

> [Levi and Simeon] slew Hamor and Shechem his son with the edge of the sword, and took Dinah out of Shechem's house, and went out. The sons of Jacob came upon the slain, and spoiled the city, because they had defiled their sister. They took their sheep, and their oxen, and their asses, and that which was in the city, and that which was in the field, and all their wealth, and all their little ones, and their wives took they captive, and spoiled even all that was in the house. (Gen. 34:26–29)

> Simeon and Levi are brethren; instruments of cruelty are in their habitations. O my soul, come not thou into their secret; unto their assembly, mine honour, be not thou united: for in their anger they slew a man, and in their selfwill they digged down a wall. Cursed be their anger, for it was fierce; and their wrath, for it was cruel: I will divide them in Jacob, and scatter them in Israel. (Gen. 49:5–7)

That wrath tends to be a disposition or character trait appears in God's denunciation of the Edomites. The capital sin of wrath is not an isolated and properly utilized force for redressing injustices.

> Thus saith the Lord; For three transgressions of Edom, and for four, I will not turn away the punishment thereof; because he did pursue his brother with the sword, and did cast off all pity, and his anger did tear perpetually, and he kept his wrath for ever. (Amos 1:11)

Wrath frequently misfires. Because we don't take the time to sort through guilt and innocence properly—both in reference to the guilty party and the measure of guilt—we direct our wrath at the wrong people in the wrong situations. This happened to Joseph. If Potiphar had really believed that Joseph was guilty of seduction, he probably would have executed Joseph. But Potiphar's wrath, once aroused, demanded venting. He couldn't destroy his wife; so he directed it elsewhere, and the innocent became guilty according to wrath's verdict.

> And it came to pass, when his master heard the words of his wife, which she spake unto him, saying, After this manner did thy servant to me; that his wrath was kindled. And Joseph's master took him, and put him into the prison, a place where the king's prisoners were bound. (Gen. 39:19–20)

God knows all of these defects in wrath. He knows that there are times when His people will correctly identify injustice, will correctly recognize the guilty individuals, but will be so stirred up with anger that they might swerve away from a just solution. We see wickedness all around us. We see it entrenched in the highest levels of our government. We see the greedy, envious, and lustful prospering. They even get laws passed to support and defend their wickedness against the righteous. This is unjust. We recognize it. We can put names and faces to presidents, Supreme Court justices, senators, representatives, governors, financiers, and others who have devoted themselves to the overthrow of God's law and His people. So what are we to do? Our anger is legitimately stirred by such injustice. But we must heed the Word of our God lest, carried away by anger, we act in ways that are disobedient, vindictive, and unjust. God comforted the psalmist who faced the same problem of evil that we face today:

> Rest in the Lord, and wait patiently for him: fret not thyself because of him who prospereth in his way, because of the man who bringeth wicked devices to pass. Cease from anger, and forsake wrath: fret not thyself in any wise to do evil. For evildoers shall be cut off: but those that wait upon the Lord, they shall inherit the earth. (Ps. 37:7–9)

One phrase in 37:8 is a bit awkward: "Fret not thyself in any wise to do evil." This phrase can also be translated "Fret not yourself; it tends only to evil" (ESV) or "Do not fret, it leads only to evildoing" (NASB). In other words, a biblically-informed sense of justice can actually lead to evil when wrath takes the helm of our lives. God alone exercises wrath in perfect measure toward the guilty. We have the privilege of yielding our anger to Him so that it doesn't fester and mutate into the sin of wrath (Eph. 4:26).

INTERCONNECTIONS WITH OTHER SINS

Like the other capital sins, anger keeps poor company. It occurs in several vice lists closely connected with a series of destructive sins.

Let all bitterness, and wrath, and anger, and clamour, and evil speaking, be put away from you, with all malice. (Eph. 4:31)

Also put off all these; anger, wrath, malice, blasphemy, filthy communication out of your mouth. Lie not one to another, seeing that ye have put off the old man with his deeds. (Col. 3:8–9)

Wrath tends to connect very closely with selfishness and pride. Jerry Bridges has observed, "Someone else's words or actions may become the occasion of our anger, but the cause lies deep within us—usually our pride, or selfishness, or desire to control."[6] If our own pride weren't at stake, we could be impartially concerned about justice. But we wield excessive force and demand excessive repayment from those who have offended, frustrated, or hurt us because they have offended *us* as opposed to someone else. Often, since we cannot actually hurt the ones who have offended us, we direct our wrath against innocent victims. For example, none of those who died in the shootings in Aurora, Sandy Hook, and Lafayette had offended their murderers. But these murderers allowed frustration and wounded pride to cloud their judgment to the point that they vented their wrath on people who had never offended or harmed them in any way.[7]

Even in lampooning the seriousness of anger, Robert Thurman admits that "anger causes the breaking of these [Jewish and

---

[6] Jerry Bridges, *Respectable Sins: Confronting the Sins We Tolerate* (Colorado Springs: NavPress, 2007), 122.

[7] Stevens and Ung agree, "Of all our emotions, anger is the most explosive, often raw-edged, and a catalyst for other destructive forces such as envy, pride, depression, and even murder." Paul R. Stevens and Alvin Ung, *Taking Your Soul to Work: Overcoming the Nine Deadly Sins of the Workplace* (Grand Rapids: Eerdmans, 2010), 40–41.

Christian ethical] codes, causes killing, slander, maliciousness."[8] When someone receives something that we think we deserve just as much or more, envy stirs our anger. Israel's anger in response to the Gentiles' reception of the gospel in the New Testament derived from envy.

> But I say, Did not Israel know? First Moses saith, I will provoke you to jealousy by them that are no people, and by a foolish nation I will anger you. (Rom. 10:19)

The passages covered in the previous section show us that wrath can lead to conspiracies, false imprisonment, murder, greed and theft, kidnapping, and slavery. We can hide our anger for a while, but even if we suppress it internally, it wreaks havoc. "As overt hostility and revengefulness are considered unbecoming of those who have chosen the Christian ministry as their profession, we suspect that much of this anger gets internalized as 'inner rage,' and it is now quite well established that such rage often manifests itself in the form of depression or of fatigue . . . or in behavior that places one's ministerial position in jeopardy (for example, sexual and financial misconduct)," say Capps and Cole.[9] They conclude that anger can lead to at least three other capital sins: sloth, lust, and greed.[10] Suppression is not the solution. We have to surrender to the Lord the right to judge and condemn. We can still stand for righteousness, truth, and other virtues without taking on ourselves the mantle of judge and executioner. Surrendering our anger to the

---

[8] Robert A. F. Thurman, *Anger: The Seven Deadly Sins* (Oxford: University Press, 2005), 19.

[9] Donald Capps and Allan Hugh Cole Jr., "The Deadly Sins and Saving Virtues: How They Are Viewed Today by Clergy," *Pastoral Psychology* 54 (2006): 534.

[10] Steven James concurs with the interplay of anger and at least one initial stage of sloth, namely, doubt: "Sometimes doubt leads to anger; sometimes anger leads to doubt. But neither leads to peace." *Flirting with the Forbidden: Finding Grace in a World of Temptation* (Grand Rapids: Revell, 2012), 46.

Lord brings us peace and short-circuits the damage that it causes through its connections with so many other destructive sins.

Nebuchadnezzar, the king of Babylon who conquered Jerusalem, repeatedly exhibited wrath whenever his will was thwarted. His anger turned him against faithful servants with the result that he falsely accused them of betrayal when his own prideful behavior was actually the problem. In his anger he insulted God (much as Sennacherib had done many years earlier; cf. 2 Kings 19:27–28, which specifically attributes an attack on God to anger). His anger led to the unnecessary death of some of his soldiers.

TABLE 8.1: SINS CONNECTED WITH WRATH—THE LIFE OF NEBUCHADNEZZAR

Daniel	Verse	Sin
3:15	If ye worship not, ye shall be cast the same hour into the midst of a burning fiery furnace; and who is that God that shall deliver you out of my hands?	impiety, blasphemy
3:19	Then was Nebuchadnezzar full of fury, and the form of his visage was changed against Shadrach, Meshach, and Abednego.	unwarranted shift of favor
3:19, 22	Therefore he spake, and commanded that they should heat the furnace one seven times more than it was wont to be heated. . . . Therefore because the king's commandment was urgent, and the furnace exceeding hot, the flame of the fire slew those men that took up Shadrach, Meshach, and Abednego.	irrational and destructive behavior

Many other passages connect unrestrained anger with other sins. In particular, these passages show us that envy and pride regularly motivate wrath. And disobedience, false imprisonment, abusive speech, and murder often result from wrath.

TABLE 8.2: SINS CONNECTED WITH WRATH—OTHER SCRIPTURES

Reference	Verse	Sin
Genesis 4:5, 8	And Cain was very wroth . . . and it came to pass, when they were in the field, that Cain rose up against Abel his brother, and slew him.	envy, murder
1 Samuel 18:8–11	And Saul was very wroth, and the saying displeased him; and he said, They have ascribed unto David ten thousands, and to me they have ascribed but thousands: and what can he have more but the kingdom? And Saul eyed David from that day and forward. . . . And there was a javelin in Saul's hand. And Saul cast the javelin; for he said, I will smite David even to the wall with it.	
Matthew 2:16	Then Herod, when he saw that he was mocked of the wise men, was exceeding wroth, and sent forth, and slew all the children that were in Bethlehem, and in all the coasts thereof, from two years old and under, according to the time which he had diligently enquired of the wise men.	

Reference	Verse	Sin
2 Kings 5:11–12	But Naaman was wroth, and went away, and said, Behold, I thought, He will surely come out to me, and stand, and call on the name of the Lord his God, and strike his hand over the place, and recover the leper. Are not Abana and Pharpar, rivers of Damascus, better than all the waters of Israel? may I not wash in them, and be clean? So he turned and went away in a rage.	pride, disobedience
2 Chronicles 26:18–19	And they withstood Uzziah the king, and said unto him, It appertaineth not unto thee, Uzziah, to burn incense unto the Lord, but to the priests the sons of Aaron, that are consecrated to burn incense: go out of the sanctuary; for thou hast trespassed; neither shall it be for thine honour from the Lord God. Then Uzziah was wroth, and had a censer in his hand to burn incense: and while he was wroth with the priests, the leprosy even rose up in his forehead before the priests in the house of the Lord.	
2 Chronicles 16:10, 12	Then Asa was wroth with the seer, and put him in a prison house; for he was in a rage with him because of this thing. And Asa oppressed some of the people the same time. . . . And Asa in the thirty and ninth year of his reign was diseased in his feet, until his disease was exceeding great: yet in his disease he sought not to the Lord, but to the physicians.	false imprisonment, injustice, attacking God's people, oppression, self-reliance
Jeremiah 37:15–16	Wherefore the princes were wroth with Jeremiah, and smote him, and put him in prison in the house of Jonathan the scribe: for they had made that the prison. . . . Jeremiah was entered into the dungeon, and into the cabins, and Jeremiah had remained there many days.	

Reference	Verse	Sin
Nehemiah 4:1, 7–8	But it came to pass, that when Sanballat heard that we builded the wall, he was wroth, and took great indignation, and mocked the Jews. . . . But it came to pass, that when Sanballat, and Tobiah, and the Arabians, and the Ammonites, and the Ashdodites, heard that the walls of Jerusalem were made up, and that the breaches began to be stopped, then they were very wroth, And conspired all of them together to come and to fight against Jerusalem, and to hinder it.	mockery, conspiracy to destroy
Revelation 12:17	And the dragon was wroth with the woman, and went to make war with the remnant of her seed, which keep the commandments of God, and have the testimony of Jesus Christ.	irrational war against God

WRATH TODAY

The Bible's depiction of wrath's attendant sins cautions us against acting hastily in anger. Offenses abound in this world. We all suffer misunderstanding, mistreatment, and outright injustice from parents, siblings, teachers, coworkers, employers, government officials, and even people that we chance to meet on the road. Surrounded by injustice, frustration, and suffering, we might cultivate a hair-trigger temper that's quick to take offense, swift to retaliate, and incautious in discerning both the nature and gravity of the offenses against us.

Road rage illustrates the intemperate nature of wrath perfectly. An offense, real or imagined, pricks one's pride. Pride magnifies the offense so that it becomes a calculated, malicious injustice in our eyes. Of course, we stand for justice; so we seek to rectify the injustice (retaliate). And all manner of cursing, reckless behavior, escalation into violence, and even murder can follow. How many sins attend this simple incident that may have taken only a minute to unfold in real time? Pride, selfishness, hatred toward humanity, recklessness, cursing, real injustice, and injury—all these sins connect with our wrath.

Frustrations at work lead to wrath at home as the innocent victims, usually a wife and children, experience the out-of-control behavior of a husband and father. Those who have done nothing wrong suffer unjustified, destructive wrath. The man of the house might be angry at something that happened at work, but he destroys the sanctity of his own home with his wrath. His wrath produces abusive speech, unkindness, and selfishness at least, and it can lead to battery, lies to cover the abuse, and even murder. Henry Fairlie observes, "In its turn Wrath will inflame the other sins. The angry man is likely to become more proud, more envious, more avaricious, and he may even become more slothful, attending less than he should to other things, since his Wrath consumes him."[11]

> *Surrendering our anger to the Lord brings us peace and short-circuits the damage that it causes through its connections with so many other destructive sins.*

When we become angry, we should set our minds quickly on the things of the Spirit. Most of our anger is ill-conceived and leads to other evils.[12] In those cases where there may actually have been an

---

[11] Henry, Fairlie, *The Seven Deadly Sins Today* (Washington, DC: New Republic Books, 1978), 89.

[12] Karl. A. Olsson observes, "Paradoxical as it seems, most anger is sinful. It is sinful not because the emotion itself is wrong but because the thing we want is wrong or we are angry at the wrong person or in the wrong way or for too long a time. Perhaps we can say that human anger is always perverted by sin and instead of burning, like the divine wrath, with a clean flame, it generates a blinding and suffocating smoke. It is thus that Dante saw anger, and it is thus that we see it most frequently in ourselves." *Seven Sins and Seven Virtues* (New York: Harper & Brothers, 1959), 29.

offense, we need not assume the worst of others nor magnify the severity of the injustice incurred. We must also consider the grace that we've received in our daily, hourly offenses against the justice of God. We should look for practical ways to extend kindness and love to others lest we find ourselves caught in a web of vice. When we release our hurt, frustration, and suffering of injustice to God, we keep our legitimate anger from turning into the settled disposition of wrath. We yield to the perfect Judge the right to try our case, and we set before our Father our frustrations and sufferings so that He can fill us with His peace.

We also face the grim reality that our world is becoming increasingly wrathful toward Christians because it is increasingly hostile toward God. One of the primary (irrational) responses of angry government officials is a false imprisonment of people who are actually quite loyal. God has called us to peace. He has commanded us to obey the ruling authorities since He is the one who sets in place those who govern and unseats them from office (Dan. 4:17, 25). Like Shadrach, Meshach, and Abednego, we cannot obey a government decree that directly contradicts God, but otherwise the tenor of our lives must be faithful obedience. Yet our obedience to God will seem recalcitrant, stubborn, and rebellious to those who would dispense with divine authority in favor of their own. On the basis of scriptural authority, we believers must prepare our hearts to experience false accusation and injustice at the hands of an angry world without giving ourselves up to the capital sin of wrath (1 Pet. 2:20–25).

God has willed that we prepare our hearts and minds through the Scriptures, recognizing where wrath will lead us, so that we don't find ourselves ensnared in a web of sin and its consequences.

9

Beyond the Capital Sins

Vice is a web spun by the spider of our own corrupt nature. This web is as extensive as our depravity, whose grip on our souls we can strengthen by both conscious and unconscious choices. Some people plunge recklessly and heedlessly into sin. They willfully add strands to the web that already ensnares their souls. Others ignore the web and pretend that they are free and untouched by sin. Denial solves nothing. The spider of corruption never sleeps.

Seven sinful dispositions radiate outwards as the main strands of the web of vice. They all connect with each other. They can all cause each other. They can all result from each other. Other sins are merely a step away when we justify, defend, or ignore the sins within us.

- Envy is preoccupied with others as undeserving of pleasure.
- Pride is preoccupied with self as deserving of pleasure.
- Sloth is preoccupied with the hopelessness of obtaining pleasure.
- Greed is preoccupied with the acquisition of things for pleasure.
- Gluttony is preoccupied with the consumption of things for pleasure.
- Lust is preoccupied with the experiencing of sensual thrills for pleasure.

- Wrath is preoccupied with hurt as undermining pleasure.

Up to this point, we haven't discussed the reason people argue over the *ultimate sin* that is the source of all the rest, but I suspect that by now you know the answer. Different authors point to pride, selfishness, corrupted love, or greed as the most basic sin because sin is so intertwined. When Adam and Eve disobeyed God in the Garden of Eden, they didn't commit merely a single sin. Pride, selfishness, unbelief, sloth, gluttony, and greed were all operating together. Teasing apart these strands of sin in the attempt to discern the "first sin" may not be as helpful as recognizing the part that they play in a complex web of disobedience to God. We fight them as a whole—hiding none, excusing none—just as we would sweep away an entire spider's web at once.

To explore the remaining connections between the known sins would take a lifetime of work and a library of documentation, but God has indicated the existence of enough connections to finalize our case: Sin is (virtually) never a single, isolated act.[1] It's a complex web of evil dispositions and evil deeds that ensnares our hearts.

---

[1] Going into greater detail does not further establish the point being made: sins are interconnected. Initially, I articulated all of the following sins in Scripture but found that their interconnections were so numerous and redundant that focusing on the seven capital sins would suffice. My original list included *malevolence* (including bitterness, brutality, savagery, cruelty, contention, dissension, dishonoring authorities, jealousy, extortion, injustice, malice, ill will, mercilessness, slander, evil speaking, unkindness, vengeance, violence, wrath, and angry outbursts), *godlessness* (including blasphemy, disobedience, idolatry, impurity, uncleanness, indifference, sorcery, unbelief, and doubt), *immorality* (including adultery, coarse talking, double entendre, fornication of any type, impure thinking, incest, and sodomy), *negligence* (including apathy, ennui, indifference, inhospitality, and laziness), *selfishness* (including ambition, arrogance, boasting, vanity, covetousness, dissolution, dissipation, drunkenness, fear, cowardice, ingratitude, revelry/partying, self-justification, theft, stealing, robbery), and *untruth* (including false teaching, apostasy, lying, scorning, mocking the truth, seduction, and urging others to do evil). The reader can see at once why a prohibitively long book would have resulted from such a list. Hopefully, we also recognize how these, in fact, relate to one or more of the capital sins already covered!

ANTITHESES

While the purpose and limitations of this book have riveted our attention on exploring a web of iniquity, there exists in God's design an even more powerful web of virtue. Since *web* conjures up negative images, we might shift into a cognate idea and call this a tapestry of virtue. Many commentators have observed that the fruit (singular) of the Spirit is love, joy, peace, longsuffering, gentleness, goodness, faith, meekness, and self-control (plural). These virtues make a single tapestry, strengthening and beautifying each other and the whole. To the extent that we become more loving, we'll also be more joyful, peaceful, and good. As our faith increases, so will our patience and gentleness. We cannot grow in one aspect of our sanctification without becoming more mature throughout the whole of our spiritual life. And this is a great encouragement. When we read certain passages of Scripture, we might misunderstand their instruction and assume that we must fix one area of life before moving on to another. Peter presents such a list:

> *Sin is (virtually) never a single, isolated act. It's a complex web of evil dispositions and evil deeds that ensnares our hearts.*

> For this very reason, make every effort to supplement your faith with virtue, and virtue with knowledge, and knowledge with self-control, and self-control with steadfastness, and steadfastness with godliness, and godliness with brotherly affection, and brotherly affection with love. (2 Pet. 1:5–7, ESV)

That the passage isn't teaching a sequential adding of one thing to another, but a weaving together of complementary elements stems from the two verses that follow the list. Peter believes that all these qualities are already present in the believers and are continuing to increase. He expects believers to "supplement" each aspect of sanctification with each of the other aspects!

> For if these qualities are yours and are increasing, they keep
> you from being ineffective or unfruitful in the knowledge
> of our Lord Jesus Christ. For whoever lacks these qualities
> is so nearsighted that he is blind, having forgotten that he
> was cleansed from his former sins. (2 Pet. 1:8–9, ESV)

Sin often seems inescapably present and relentlessly powerful in our lives. But through the grace of God at work in us by His Spirit, virtue is more inescapably present and more relentlessly powerful. And so we build in hope because the work of God is exactly that—His work—which He will perfect and complete in the day of Christ. Table 9.1 shows us the virtues that God is working in us to overthrow the web of vice that enshrouds our lives.

TABLE 9.1: THE TAPESTRY OF VIRTUES

Seven Vices	Seven Virtues	Key Passage
envy (*invidia*)	kindness (*humanitas*)	Put on therefore, as the elect of God, holy and beloved, bowels of mercies, kindness, humbleness of mind, meekness, longsuffering; forbearing one another, and forgiving one another, if any man have a quarrel against any: even as Christ forgave you, so also do ye. (Col. 3:12–13)
pride (*superbia*)	humility (*humilitas*)	Yea, all of you be subject one to another, and be clothed with humility: for God resisteth the proud, and giveth grace to the humble. (1 Pet. 5:5)

Seven Vices	Seven Virtues	Key Passage
sloth (*acedia*)	diligence (*industria*)	And we desire that every one of you do shew the same diligence to the full assurance of hope unto the end: that ye be not slothful, but followers of them who through faith and patience inherit the promises. (Heb. 6:11–12)
greed (*avaritia*)	charity (*caritas*)	Let him labour, working with his hands the thing which is good, that he may have to give to him that needeth. (Eph. 4:28) Charity suffereth long, and is kind; charity envieth not; charity vaunteth not itself, is not puffed up, doth not behave itself unseemly, seeketh not her own, is not easily provoked, thinketh no evil; rejoiceth not in iniquity, but rejoiceth in the truth; beareth all things, believeth all things, hopeth all things, endureth all things. (1 Cor. 13:4–7)[1]
gluttony (*gula*)	temperance (*temperantia*)	Beside this, giving all diligence, add to your faith virtue; and to virtue knowledge; and to knowledge temperance; and to temperance patience; and to patience godliness; and to godliness brotherly kindness; and to brotherly kindness charity. (2 Pet. 1:5–7)
lust (*luxuria*)	chastity (*castitas*)	Flee also youthful lusts: but follow righteousness, faith, charity, peace, with them that call on the Lord out of a pure heart. (2 Tim. 2:22, cf. 1 Tim. 4:12; 5:2)
wrath (*ira*)	patience (*patientia*)[2]	[We are] remembering without ceasing your work of faith, and labour of love, and patience of hope in our Lord Jesus Christ, in the sight of God and our Father. (1 Thess. 1:3)

Notice how many of these passages list the virtues in close conjunction with each other. As we become what God wants us to become in one area of life, we progress in the sanctification that strengthens all the virtues.

CONCLUSION

Sin is serious. If we trust God at all, we cannot hear passages such as 1 Corinthians 6:9–10 without being sobered by them:

> Be not deceived: neither fornicators, nor idolaters, nor adulterers, nor effeminate, nor abusers of themselves with mankind, nor thieves, nor covetous, nor drunkards, nor revilers, nor extortioners, shall inherit the kingdom of God.

This single passage directly addresses three of the capital sins (lust, greed, and gluttony). It reminds us of the interconnectedness of sin and encourages a healthy spiritual self-examination concerning our faith. "The scriptures know nothing of that kind of confidence which renders men easy in their sins."[2]

We struggle with sin, in part, because we cannot always identify the source of our sin. Every pastor has dealt with the man who divorces his wife, the college student who quits church, or the businessman who was caught embezzling from his company. All these sins seem to occur suddenly and without warning.

We cannot grow in one aspect of our sanctification without becoming more mature throughout the whole of our spiritual life.

Shock ripples through the church because we didn't see these tragic events coming. We don't always recognize core vices that lead to other sins. We don't realize that small sins lead to other sins. And so we are surprised.

---

[2] Andrew Fuller, *The Backslider: His Nature, Symptoms, and Means for Recovery* (1801; repr., Birmingham: Solid Ground Christian Books, 2005), 20.

We're shocked when we hear about a murder, but we never consider that murder might spring from any one of the capital vices.

- Envy—Cain killed Abel over the honor Abel received from God (Gen. 4:8).

- Pride—Lamech killed a man for simply offending him (Gen. 4:23).

- Sloth—Jehoram tried to kill Elisha because of discouragement over the siege and resulting famine in the land (2 Kings 6:30–33).

- Greed—Ahab killed Naboth for a vineyard (1 Kings 21:1–13).

- Gluttony—The leaders of Israel killed people to glut themselves (Ezek. 34:1–3).

- Lust—David killed Uriah to conceal David's adulterous relationship with Bathsheba (2 Sam. 11:14–17, 12:9).

- Wrath—Moses killed an Egyptian in anger over his treatment of a Hebrew slave (Exod. 2:11–12).

So when we tolerate any vice, we're tolerating the very strands of the web of inquity that can lead to *any* other sin—even the most horrific sins.[3]

Ministers should be on guard to identify what's really happening in the life of the congregation. A man doesn't simply divorce his wife one day. He has nursed envy, lust, anger, or some other sin for some time. A college student doesn't quit church on a whim. He has become embittered through an offense against his pride, or he has become proud through his negligent sloth.

---

[3] Mark R. McMinn, *Why Sin Matters: The Surprising Relationship Between Our Sin and God's Grace* (Wheaton: Tyndale House, 2004), 88.

God's Word forces us to analyze our lives: what's really at the root of our "trivial" behaviors? Ministers must be especially careful not to trivialize "minor" sins that are cropping up in their personal lives. Ministerial failure is profound and shocking. Far too many believers who seem "too big to fail" find their character and ministries compromised due to a lack of personal analysis and serious efforts to eradicate sin.

A morbid fascination with sin and its inner workings doesn't sanctify, nor does Scripture require us to probe every conceivable sin in our nature in order to receive forgiveness and restoration. In fact, "the heart is more deceitful than all else and is desperately sick; who can understand it?" (Jer. 17:9, NASB). That's the reason this book isn't designed to encourage the

> *As the insect caught in a web cannot escape by his own striving, we cannot escape the web of our sin on our own.*

reader to root out of himself, by himself, every trace of sin. Rather, it's intended to help us address situations in which we haven't gotten victory, at least in part, due to some deep root of sin that we're unaware of. It reminds us that our sin is a web of tremendous proportions, and if we leave the strands of the web intact, they will become the scaffold for new sins. It addresses the self-assured man who thinks he's beyond sin simply because he cannot point to any recent instance of major, external sin. It addresses the hurting person who thinks that forgiveness is impossible—the snare is too great. In Christ, the web is torn. Its tattered threads blow idly. We are snared for a moment more in this life only, and then we enter into the great liberty that He has won. Finally, this book addresses those who long to magnify God's grace but whose avoidance of the topic of sin ultimately debases that very grace by minimizing its significance. Grace is so great because sin is so great.

I walked outside my back door and glanced up. Yes, my wife was right. She had told me that the number of spider webs on the porch had increased to "critical mass." "No, there can't be that many," I had said. "I walk through that door every day, and I haven't seen them." Apparently I hadn't been looking. Webs were everywhere. I'm not particularly squeamish, but I draw the line at clearing out spider webs with my bare hands. I went for a broom. In minutes the back porch was pristine and web-free. True, they'll be back again next week. They always accumulate on the sly, but my broom is ready by the door. Can I reasonably do less than this with the sin in my life?

The Holy Spirit wields the broom of His Word in our lives, relentlessly clearing out the webs of our sin. When we submit to His will and walk in His strength, He sweeps out the sin that ensnares us. We don't want to manage our sin; we want to be free from it. But, as the insect caught in a web cannot escape by his own striving, we cannot escape the web of our sin on our own. Struggle results in further injury but not in freedom. Deliverance comes through one who is powerful enough to sweep out this web of iniquity and set us free. We concur with the reflections of the apostle Paul. Who can cut the strands of sin in my life and sweep out the web of vice?

> But I see another law in my members, warring against the law of my mind, and bringing me into captivity to the law of sin which is in my members. O wretched man that I am! who shall deliver me from the body of this death? I thank God through Jesus Christ our Lord. (Rom. 7:23–25)

We echo these words of praise because God, in Christ, has exposed and cut sin's web so that we might be free.

> Sweep out my soul, O Lord; too long sin's snare
> Has spun its silken cord across my heart.
> It shimmered in the dew of dawn and seemed
> So innocent, so soft, so beautiful.
> I saw the threat too late to extricate
> My soul. I touched a single strand that held
> No peril—only promise—in its form
> And found it pleasant till I would withdraw.
> Alas, it would not yield! The more I fought,
> The more entangled I became, for sin
> Unites with sin to trap unwary prey—
> wrath, envy, lust, greed, pride, sloth, gluttony.
> Sweep out my soul, O Lord; deliver me.
> Cut sin's dark web, and set Your servant free.

BIBLIOGRAPHY

Anderson, Neil T. and Joanne Anderson. *Overcoming Depression*. Ventura, CA: Regal Books, 2004.

Arterburn, Stephen and Debra Cherry. *Take Control of What's Controlling You: A Guide to Personal Freedom*. Nashville: Integrity House, 2006.

Auden, W. H. "On Anger." In *The Seven Deadly Sins*, 78–87. Edited by Ian Fleming. New York: William Morrow and Company, 1962.

Backus, William. *What Your Counselor Never Told You: Seven Secrets Revealed— Conquer the Power of Sin in Your Life*. Minneapolis: Bethany House, 2000.

Baughman, Michael. *Money Sucks: A Memoir on Why Too Much or Too Little Can Ruin You*. New York: Skyhorse Publishing, 2014.

Beecher, Marguerite and Willard Beecher. *The Mark of Cain: An Anatomy of Jealousy*. New York: Harper & Row Publishers, 1971.

Bevere, Lisa. *Kissed the Girls and Made Them Cry: Why Women Lose When They Give In*. Nashville: Thomas Nelson, 2002.

Bolton, Robert. *The Carnal Professor: Discovering the Woeful Slavery of a Man Guided by the Flesh*. 1634. Reprint, Ligonier, PA: Soli Deo Gloria Publications, 1992.

Bridges, Jerry. *Respectable Sins: Confronting the Sins We Tolerate*. Colorado Springs: NavPress, 2007.

Burroughs, Jeremiah. *The Evil of Evils, or the Exceeding Sinfulness of Sin*. 1654. Reprint, Morgan, PA: Soli Deo Gloria Publications, 1992.

Burton, Marion Le Roy. *The Problem of Evil: A Criticism of the Augustinian Point of View*. Chicago: Open Court Publishing Company, 1909.

Capps, Donald, and Allan Hugh Cole Jr. "The Deadly Sins and Saving Virtues: How They Are Viewed Today by Clergy." *Pastoral Psychology* 54 (2006): 517–34.

Capps, Donald, and Melissa Haupt. "The Deadly Sins: How They Are Viewed and Experienced Today." *Pastoral Psychology* 60 (2011): 791–807.

Cassian, John. *The Works of John Cassian*, vol. 11 of *A Select Library of the Nicene and Post-Nicene Fathers of the Christian Church*. Translated by Edgar C. S. Gibson; edited by Philip Schaff and Henry Wace. Buffalo, NY: Christian Literature Publishing Company, 1894. http://biblehub.com/library/cassian/the_works_of_john_cassian_/chapter_vii_of_the_source.htm.

Chan, Tina. "Review of Simon Laham, *The Science of Sin: The Psychology of the Seven Deadlies (and Why They Are So Good for You)*." *Library Journal* 137, no. 2 (Feb. 2012): 79–80.

Clapp, Rodney, ed. *The Consuming Passion: Christianity and the Consumer Culture*. Downers Grove, IL: InterVarsity Press, 1998.

Cohn, Alicia. "Grace amid the Vices: Exploring the Seven Deadly Sin's Doesn't Have to Be Depressing—Interview of Rebecca Kondyck DeYoung." *Christianity Today*, September 2009, 84.

Davidson, William L. "Envy and Emulation." In *Encyclopedia of Religion and Ethics*, vol. 5. Edited by James Hastings. New York: Charles Scribner's Sons, 1912.

DeYoung, Rebecca Konyndyk. *Glittering Vices: A New Look at the Seven Deadly Sins and Their Remedies*. Grand Rapids: Brazos Press, 2009.

———. *Vainglory: The Forgotten Vice*. Grand Rapids: William B. Eerdmans Publishing Company, 2014.

Dime, Cysa. *How to Offend God and Suffer the Consequences in Seven Easy Lessons: Or the Seven Deadly Sins*. Crane, MO: Highway, 2009.

Dixon, Jim. *Vice and Virtue: The Battle Within*. Boulder, CO: Johnson's Printing, 2001.

Dyson, Michael Eric. *Pride: The Seven Deadly Sins*. Oxford: Oxford University Press, 2006.

Epstein, Joseph. *Envy: The Seven Deadly Sins*. Oxford: Oxford University Press, 2003.

Everts, Don. *The Smell of Sin and the Fresh Air of Grace*. Downers Grove, IL: InterVarsity Press, 2003.

Ezell, Rick. *The Seven Sins of Highly Defective People*. Grand Rapids: Kregel, 2003.

Fairlie, Henry. *The Seven Deadly Sins Today*. Washington, DC: New Republic Books, 1978.

Farber, Leslie H. "Faces of Envy." In *The Virtues: Contemporary Essays on Moral Character*. Edited by Robert B. Kruschwitz and Robert C. Roberts. Belmont, CA: Wadsworth Publishing Company, 1987.

Flavel, John. *Triumphing Over Sinful Fear*. Edited by J. Stephen Yuille. Puritan Treasures for Today series. Edited by Joel R. Beeke and Jay T. Collier. 1682. Reprint, Grand Rapids: Reformation Heritage Books, 2011.

Fleming, Ian, ed. *The Seven Deadly Sins*. By Angus Wilson, Edith Sitwell, Cyril Connolly, Patrick Fermor, Evelyn Waugh, Christopher Sykes, and W. H. Auden. New York: William Morrow and Company, 1962.

Frank, Lisa. "The Evolution of the Seven Deadly Sins: From God to the Simpsons." *Journal of Popular Culture* 35 (2001): 95–105.

Fuller, Andrew. *The Backslider: His Nature, Symptoms, and Means for Recovery*. 1801. Reprint, Birmingham: Solid Ground Christian Books, 2005.

Graham, Billy. *The Seven Deadly Sins.* Grand Rapids: Zondervan Publishing House, 1955.

Hall, Laurie. *An Affair of the Mind: One Woman's Courageous Battle to Salvage Her Family from the Devastation of Pornography.* Colorado Springs: Focus on the Family Publishing, 1996.

Harris, John. *Mammon; or, Covetousness the Sin of the Christian Church.* 1836. Reprint, Swengel, PA: Bible Truth Depot, 1959.

Harris, Joshua. *Not Even a Hint.* Sisters, OR: Multnomah, 2003.

Hawkins, Emma B. "Tolkien's Linguistic Application of the Seventh Deadly Sin: Lust." *Mythlore* 26, nos. 3–4 (2008): 29–40.

Henderson, Daniel. *Think Before You Look: Avoiding the Consequences of Secret Temptation.* Chattanooga: Ink Books, 2005.

Houston, James. M., ed. *Sin and Temptation: The Challenge of Personal Godliness.* Adapted from *The Works of John Owen.* 1983. Reprint, Minneapolis: Bethany House Publishers, 1996.

Hummel, Rand. *Turn Away Wrath: Meditations to Control Anger and Bitterness.* Greenville, SC: JourneyForth, 2007.

Hunt, June. *Keeping Your Cool When Your Anger Is Hot: Practical Steps to Temper Fiery Emotions.* Eugene, OR: Harvest House Publishers, 2009.

James, Steven. *Flirting with the Forbidden: Finding Grace in a World of Temptation.* Grand Rapids: Revell, 2012.

Keizer, Garret. *The Enigma of Anger: Essays on a Sometimes Deadly Sin.* San Francisco: Jossey-Bass, 2002.

Keller, Timothy. *Counterfeit Gods: The Empty Promises of Money, Sex, and Power, and the Only Hope That Matters.* London: Dutton, 2009.

Knight, James A. *For the Love of Money: Human Behavior and Money.* Philadelphia: J. B. Lippincott Company, 1968.

Komp, Diane M. *Anatomy of a Lie: The Truth About Lies and Why Good People Tell Them.* Grand Rapids: Zondervan, 1998.

LaMothe, Ryan. "Sloth and Pastoral Counseling." *Journal of Spirituality in Mental Health* 9, no. 2 (2006): 3–25.

Lewis, C. S. *The Abolition of Man: How Education Develops Man's Sense of Morality.* New York: MacMillan, 1947.

Ludy, Eric and Leslie. *Meet Mr. Smith: Revolutionize the Way You Think About Sex, Purity, and Romance.* Nashville: Thomas Nelson, 2007.

Lundgaard, Kris. *The Enemy Within: Straight Talk About the Power and Defeat of Sin.* Phillipsburg, NJ: P & R Publishing, 1998. [241.3 L9723, 157 pages]

Mack, Wayne A. *Humility: The Forgotten Virtue.* Phillipsburg, NJ: P&R Publishing, 2005.

Mack, Wayne A. and Joshua Mack. *A Fight to the Death: Taking Aim at Sin Within.* Phillipsburg, NJ: P&R Publishing, 2006.

Mackay, W. Mackintosh. *The Disease and Remedy of Sin*. London: Hodder and Stoughton, 1918.

Mahaney, C. J., ed. *Worldliness: Resisting the Seduction of a Fallen World*. Wheaton: Crossway, 2008.

Mangis, Michael. *Signature Sins: Taming Our Wayward Hearts*. Downers Grove, IL: InterVarsity Press Books, 2008.

McCracken, Robert J. *What Is Sin? What Is Virtue?* New York: Harper & Row, 1966.

McGowan, Kathleen. "Seven Deadly Sins." *Discover*, September 2009, http://discovermagazine.com/2009/sep/05-i-didnt-sin-it-was-my-brain.

McMinn, Mark R. *Why Sin Matters: The Surprising Relationship Between Our Sin and God's Grace*. Wheaton: Tyndale House, 2004.

Miller, J. Keith. *Sin: Overcoming the Ultimate Deadly Addiction*. San Francisco: Harper & Row, 1987.

Myers, David G. *The Inflated Self: Human Illusions and the Biblical Call to Hope*. New York: Seabury Press, 1980.

Oliver, Gary Jackson, and H. Norman Wright. *When Anger Hits Home: Taking Care of Your Anger Without Taking It Out on Your Family*. Chicago: Moody, 1992.

Olsson, Karl. A. *Seven Sins and Seven Virtues*. New York: Harper & Brothers, 1959.

Orr, James. *Sin as a Problem of Today*. London: Hodder & Stoughton, 1910.

Peters, Ted. *Sin: Radical Evil in Soul and Society*. Grand Rapids: William B. Eerdmans Publishing Company, 1994.

Prose, Francine. *Gluttony: The Seven Deadly Sins*. Oxford: Oxford University Press, 2003.

Pynchon, Thomas, Mary Gordon, John Updike, William Trevor, Gore Vidal, Richard Howard, A. S. Byatt, and Joyce Carol Oates. *Deadly Sins*. New York: William Morrow and Company, Inc., 1993.

Ramm, Bernard. *Offense to Reason: A Theology of Sin*. San Francisco: Harper & Row Publishers, 1985.

Sayers, Dorothy. *The Whimsical Christian*. 1969. Reprint, New York: Macmillan Publishing Company, Inc., 1978.

Schlumpf, Heidi. "Who's Afraid of the Seven Deadly Sins?" *U.S. Catholic* 65, no. 2 (February 2000): 22–25.

Schoeck, Helmut. *Envy: A Theory of Social Behavior*. Translated by Michael Glenny and Betty Ross. New York: Harcourt, Brace & World, Inc., 1966.

Smith, Holly. "Culpable Ignorance." *The Philosophical Review* 92, no. 4 (Oct. 1983): 543–71.

Stafford, William S. *Disordered Loves: Healing the Seven Deadly Sins*. Boston: Cowley Publications, 1994.

Stalker, James. *The Seven Cardinal Virtues.* Reprint, Eldorado, IL: Eldorado Book Shop, 1961.

————. *The Seven Deadly Sins.* New York: Dodd, Mead, & Co., 1901.

Stenstrom, Douglas M., and Mathew Curtis, "Pride, Sloth/Lust/Gluttony, Envy, Greed/Wrath: Rating the Seven Deadly Sins," *Interdisciplinary Journal of Research on Religion* 8 (2012):1–27.

Stevens, Paul R., and Alvin Ung. *Taking Your Soul to Work: Overcoming the Nine Deadly Sins of the Workplace.* Grand Rapids: Eerdmans, 2010.

Stroup, N. Wallace. *The Fact of Sin Viewed Historically and Doctrinally.* Cincinnati: Jennings and Graham, 1908.

Sullender, Scott. "The Seven Deadly Sins as a Pastoral Diagnostic System." *Pastoral Psychology* 64 (2015): 217–27.

Sykes, Christopher. "On Lust." In In *The Seven Deadly Sins*, 66–77. Edited by Ian Fleming. New York: William Morrow and Company, 1962.

Tennant, F. R. *The Concept of Sin.* Cambridge: Cambridge University Press, 1912.

Thurman, Robert A. F. *Anger: The Seven Deadly Sins.* Oxford: Oxford University Press, 2005.

Tulloch, John. *The Christian Doctrine of Sin.* New York: Scribner, Armstrong & Co., 1876.

Veselka, Livia, Erica A. Giammarco, and Philip A. Vernon. "The Dark Triad and the Seven Deadly Sins." *Personality and Individual Differences* 67 (2014): 75–80.

Wasserstein, Wendy. *Sloth: The Seven Deadly Sins.* Oxford: Oxford University Press, 2005.

Webb, Lance. *Conquering the Seven Deadly Sins.* Nashville: Abingdon Press, 1955.

White, Mel. *Lust: The Other Side of Love.* Old Tappan, NJ: Fleming H. Revell Company, 1978.

Willmer, Wesley K., and Martyn Smith. *God and Your Stuff: The Vital Link Between Your Possessions and Your Soul.* Colorado Springs: NavPress, 2002.

Scripture Index

Subject Index